# DISINFORMED

Dr. Daniel Lawrence

# DISINFORMED:

## The History Of Humanity's Search For Truth

Urano
publishing

Argentina - Chile - Colombia - Spain
USA - Mexico - Peru - Uruguay

© 2024 by Dr. Daniel Lawrence

© 2024 by Urano Publishing, an imprint of Urano World USA, Inc

8871 SW 129th Terrace Miami FL 33176 USA

## Urano
publishing

Cover art and design by Luis Tinoco

Cover copyright © Urano Publishing, an imprint of Urano World USA, Inc

The first edition of this book was published in March 2024

ISBN: 978-1-953027-37-5

E-ISBN: 978-1-953027-39-9

Printed in Colombia

Library of Cataloging-in-Publication Data

Lawrence, Daniel

1. Philosophy 2. Rhetoric

Disinformed: A History of Humanity's Search for the Truth: Dr. Daniel Lawrence

# DEDICATION
For Kendra, Nova, Fox, and Juniper.

# TABLE OF CONTENTS

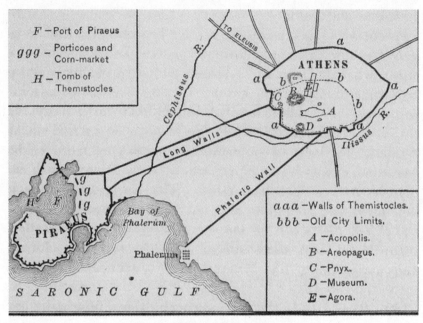

Figure 1: Map of Ancient Athens

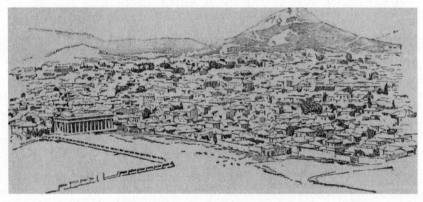

Figure 2: Drawing of Ancient Athens

Perilous to us all are the devices of an art
deeper than we possess ourselves.

J. R. R. TOLKIEN [1]

# Introduction

Well, here we are, on Earth. We're nearing the end of a global pandemic, war is ongoing in Eastern Europe, and not so long ago, a coup was attempted at the United States capitol. There's a reason the phrase "May you live in interesting times" is considered a curse.

At a time when honest, reputable information is needed most, it seems harder than ever to come by. At least 50 percent of Americans get their news from social media, while 59 percent of Americans don't trust Facebook as a reputable source of political information (according to a review of several Pew Research Center surveys conducted over the last decade). [2] Funnily enough—if you can find humor in any of this—74 percent of those surveyed by Pew did not realize that Facebook collects data about their interests and behaviors and uses this information to send them targeted advertisements, including political advertisements. I haven't written more than a few sentences, and already the disordered state of information and communication will likely be apparent to you. More than half of Americans are getting their news from a platform that more than half of Americans don't trust as a reliable source of information, while a clear majority of those users don't even understand how the platform works to deliver information to them. The trouble is not *brewing*; it has been thoroughly brewed, bottled, and delivered to our doorsteps. It is now held in the palms of our hands.

In Tolkien's fantasy classic *The Lord of the Rings*, the wizard Gandalf speaks to the hobbit Pippin about the dangers of using a technology he doesn't understand: the *palantír* or Seeing-stone. Gandalf warns, "Perilous to us all are the devices of an art deeper than we possess ourselves." [3]

The lesson is hard learned. When Pippin first picks up the palantír, he is overpowered by the dark lord Sauron and nearly reveals his knowledge about the secret quest to destroy the One Ring, a mistake which would have spelled certain disaster for Frodo and the Fellowship.

The same could be said of our current dealings with the technologies of social media and digital communications; we are dealing with an art that we do not understand, an ancient and powerful art called *persuasion*. Numerous studies indicate that we're spending more than three hours a day on mobile phones and even more time on computers—whether at home or in the workplace—but most of us don't understand how disinformation is spread across applications and platforms, and fewer still have learned the tools to decode and analyze complex digital disinformation. We are dealing with "devices of an art deeper than we possess ourselves."

When Hitler spoke, it was with an art of persuasion that his listeners did not understand, and he wove a spell over them: a dangerous, evil, and very real spell. When we are exposed to digital disinformation, we are overcome by an art deeper than we possess. But that's where this book comes in. I will show you how to analyze and evaluate the credibility of various sources of information so you can be better prepared to deal with the disinformation that invades your daily life, and I will help you learn to think like a rhetorician. I will help you to recognize this art form of persuasion—of rhetoric.

What is rhetoric? For Plato, rhetoric was matching the soul of the speaker to the soul of the listener. For Aristotle, it was the faculty of observing the available means of persuasion. For Gorgias, it was the drug-like effect that speech has on the mind, and the techniques of wielding that effect—Gorgias compared the powers of persuasion over the mind to the effects of drugs over the body.

There is no single, sufficient definition of rhetoric, and rhetoricians like to argue about the scope of the field. But I'll tell you what rhetoric is: Rhetoric is philosophy with legs. Rhetoric is the toolkit by which we create and analyze communication. Rhetoric is the art of persuasion. And we are sorely missing this lost, ancient art form in our contemporary public discourse. People in power have been lying to us for thousands of years—I'll show you in this book, for example, how King Sargon I used persuasive techniques six thousand years ago to build the world's first empire—but we have never quite caught up with the tools for decoding persuasion. Now, persuasion and disinformation come at us like a veritable storm, with the average modern citizen seeing thousands of advertisements every day. And they're not just advertisements for products, but also advertisements for political parties, advertisements disguised as opinion pieces, and straight up mis-and disinformation disguised as news and parading as reputable information.

But let's be clear: I'm not here to stir you up or cause you to panic. Quite the opposite. When I zoom out a bit, it's clear to me that humanity has always been under this threat of disinformation. Both of my grandfathers served in the United States Navy during World War II when Germany and the Axis Powers were trying to *blitzkreig* their way into world domination and much of Europe was under the spell of mass communication and propaganda. When my maternal grandfather returned from the war, he married my grandmother, and they lived in a small apartment with no hot water (a "cold water flat" as they called it). It wasn't exactly an easy life. In my parents' time, the Cold War and threat of nuclear annihilation came front and center to everyday life, as Russia began earnestly sowing discord at an international level with its powerful *dezinformatsiya* (disinformation) programs. In the early 1900s, the days of my great-grandfather Frank Lawrence, the United States began one of its first centralized, organized, formal propaganda campaigns to attempt to convince American citizens to join the Great War that was going on in Europe. Just a couple of generations earlier, America was burdened by a Civil War that nearly saw the country tear itself apart. And this is just in my own country, within the last few generations—anyone, anywhere, who reads this knows that their own family's history, and their own country's history is full of as much horror as it is heroism. Governments, companies, and powerful leaders have always been lying to the public, while the project of democracy has attempted to stabilize life for the average citizen.

When the world is going through uncertain times, we look to ease our troubles by staying abreast of what's going on around us. Older generations may have listened to the radio or read a newspaper. Then the television found its way into every home. Though it's tempting to look back on some golden age of journalistic integrity—and at certain times that could be a justifiable perspective—I know, from studying the history of these media technologies, that good, reliable information has always been hard to find. And I don't mean just in the last few decades or the last few generations. I mean that for thousands of years, as long as humans have been organizing themselves into cities, states, and empires, there have been folks who have tried to lie, persuade, and disinform others for their own benefit. So, we savor the good days, and we keep a keen and critical eye on everything we hear. Or at least we should. The problem is that we are just as susceptible to persuasion, disinformation, and "fake news" as ever before, and the democracies we've built continue to be tenuously held together by our collected efforts while the storm of disinformation rages on. The technologies of communication have created more sophisticated pathways for those in power to attempt to control and persuade us, and we are just as gullible and complacent as ever.

While Thomas Jefferson didn't actually write the words "An educated citizenry is vital requisite for our survival as a free people," it's thought to be an eloquent paraphrase of his perspectives on education. Jefferson did advocate for a "crusade against ignorance." And he proudly proclaimed, speaking of Americans in a 1787 letter to St. John de Crèvecoeur, "ours are the only farmers who can read Homer." [4] It's a spurious claim, of course, but if you brush aside the American exceptionalism, you can see what he was aiming at in these letters: a good, classical education in multiple disciplines. He wanted education to include the sciences, history, philosophy, ethics, mathematics, and languages. As a graduate of the public-education system in the U.S. United States' public-education system, I'm afraid that we're falling quite short of that ideal. And the effects of our lackluster education are rippling throughout the world.

We must be honest with ourselves. American high school seniors are frequently poor critical thinkers. A study I will later return to conducted by The Stanford History Education group found that 96 percent of high school seniors didn't see any problem with getting their information about global warming from a web page clearly marked as having been written and published by a fossil fuel company.[5] That would be like trusting a hungry fox to give you a status update about the wellbeing of the hens in your backyard chicken coop. It's what we could rightly call a major conflict of interest a major conflict of interest. If this research doesn't ring a few alarms in your head, it should at least give you some cause to stop and think.

And to my older readers: you aren't off the hook either. Researchers at Princeton found that, while most Americans don't share fake news articles on social media, the nine percent of users who regularly share fabricated news stories on Facebook are over the age of sixty-five.[6] I have a lot of faith in the abilities and talents of the upcoming generations, but they have a lot stacked against them: inflation, unaffordable housing, stagnant wages, climate crises, and rising education costs, just to name a few of the massive social and economic problems on our horizon.

Really, how can we place blame on these high school students from SHEG's study, when we have offered them little good news to read and no skills by which to evaluate truth? There was little-to-no mention of Socrates, Plato, or Aristotle in my public-school curriculum. Where was Quintilian, or Cicero? Why were Nietzsche, Heidegger, and Husserl tucked away in a dark corner of the public library and not the topic of conversation in a classroom? The generation who will someday run the world doesn't know how to evaluate credibility and is disconnected from the tools they need to ask the right questions: why should we trust this source? Is this person a credible speaker on this subject? What are their qualifications? Are they citing reliable data that has been peer-reviewed? We're living in the age of fake news and disinformation, and we're not providing adequate tools or resources to our children and our students to help them combat the onslaught of propaganda and manipulative communication they face. And it's already starting to show. We are easily persuaded, and we don't bother to evaluate the information we share and use. We read headlines without wondering who wrote them or from what quality of data. We conflate opinion with fact. And we're so busy trying to keep our lives together that we don't stop to wonder whether there's anything wrong with this.

But wait. Here's the kicker: very little of this is new. Sure, we now must contend with Twitter bots spreading made-up stories and Facebook targeting us with advertisements that are based on our belief systems and behaviors, but the root of this issue trails backward through time for thousands of years. The purpose of this book will be to take you on an adventure through time to look at this phenomenon of disinformation and misinformation—the "fake news" phenomenon—as it manifested in other times and places, to help shed light on where we are today and what we are dealing with. Fake news is nothing new. But to lie, deceive, and distort reality has always been horrendously dangerous. Today, hundreds of millions of people all over the world are convinced, manipulated, and made to believe persuasive lies and narratives for particular purposes. Those in power have always lied to us. They want us to go off to war, to vote for a particular candidate, to believe in a certain god or gods, to follow particular laws or rules, to think in certain ways, and to fall in line and shut our mouths.

But some of us go on fighting for the truth, refusing to keep our mouths shut. Socrates, the ancient Athenian philosopher, was eventually put to death for poking and prodding and asking too many questions, such as "What is justice?" and "How should a state be organized?" and for encouraging everyone around him to ask questions and dig deeper into their worlds and social structures. Hypatia, the ancient female philosopher of great renown, was also killed: she was yanked from her carriage by a Christian mob in the streets of Alexandria and quite literally pulled apart, limb by limb, for all the public to see. It's dangerous to be a thinker, sometimes. Cicero, the great Roman rhetorician, was beheaded. Fulvia, the wife of Marc Antony, is said to have held his decapitated head and stabbed his tongue repeatedly with a hair pin to take revenge against his powers of speech. It's always dangerous to go against the grain and to question whether everything you've been told your whole life is a lie. Not only is it dangerous to be a free thinker, but it's also hard on one's mental health. We don't like to admit we're wrong, and we get set in our ways easily. You can hardly blame a person—life is hard enough without constantly questioning one's own belief system and going off on existential journeys of discovery. American philosopher Dr. Cornel West reminds us of this when he tells us, channeling Socrates from Plato's *Apology*, "The *unexamined* life is not worth living. The *examined* life is painful—very, very painful."[7] The road to truth is not a comfortable one.

Despite all these dangers, however, humans have always been fighting back against the lies, corruption, and evil in the world. And sometimes we lose that battle. The decline and fall of Ancient Rome is a tremendous example. So is Rome's slow slip from being a republic to becoming an empire. Julius Caesar is a great reminder, really, of what can go wrong. Ancient Rome was one of the earliest representative democracies in the world and lasted in that state for nearly five hundred years, about twice the length of time that the United States has existed as a country thus far. And yet, after expanding and thriving as a democracy for five hundred years, Caesar's massive wealth and power, accumulated on his ten-year campaign in Gaul, inflated his ego and drove his country into a civil war that fractured the stability of the republic and sent it into a tailspin. After Caesar's death, Rome never returned to a democracy. Instead, it continued onward as an empire, and though it had rulers both tyrannical and sensible, it was never again ruled by a body elected by the citizens. There are many things at stake when we talk about lies, truth, and disinformation. Democracy is one of those things.

The purpose of this book is to take a step back from the craziness of our present world and to find some hope from the works of ancient and modern thinkers and scholars who have mapped out a reasonable set of philosophies and theories to deal with the problems of lies, deceptions, and propaganda. Humans have already invented a time-tested antidote to disinformation and misinformation, and we would do well to bring it back to the forefront of our collective consciousness as we deal with some of the most pressing, existentially threatening material realities of our day: climate change; economic and financial instability; global warfare; the seemingly irreconcilable "Culture Wars" of left vs. right in the United States and throughout Europe; an epidemic of technologically sophisticated misinformation and disinformation; and our well-founded, eroding trust in major institutions such as education and journalism. What is this antidote called? Why, it is the study of rhetoric, of course.

And my job, now, will be to lay all this out for you. Through stories from the ancient empires of the Near-East where people first wrestled with questions of truth, lies, deception, and disinformation, to the mobile phone that delivers targeted digital disinformation right into your home, we'll be exploring the ideas and lives of the rhetoricians—thinkers who worried about how we would battle the persuasive powers of language and communication.

Our democracies are fragile, and central to keeping an intact democracy is a willingness to search for and engage with the truth. Even at a personal, psychological level, we feel an almost intrinsic need to discover the truth, uncover the secrets of the universe, test our hypotheses, and adventure out into the great unknowns. Carl Sagan wrote in his *Pale Blue Dot* that we are wanderers, nomads. This is an anthropological, historical truth, and it rings true at a kind of intellectual, spiritual level. We live only a short time in this universe, like brief spectators at a play. Then, we are gone, apparently forever. But while we are here, we are driven to move, to seek, and to search. What we yearn for more than anything is truth; not delusion, lies, conspiracy, nor myth. We want to know what *really* happened and what's *really* going on. Where am I, what am I, and what does all this mean? Of course, I don't have those answers. But what I can offer is a method to help you evaluate whether people are onto something true, or whether people are trying to deceive you.

DR. DANIEL WILLIAM LAWRENCE

The effect of speech upon the condition
of the soul is comparable to the power
of drugs over the nature of bodies.

—GORGIAS [8]

## CHAPTER I

# What is Truth?

*All who have and do persuade people of things do so by*
*molding a false argument.*

—GORGIAS [9]

## WHO CAN WE TRUST?

It's hard to know who to trust and where to get reliable information. Americans, for example, might be more inclined to trust modern large news organizations (like CNN, MSNBC, or Fox News), than citizens of other countries are to trust their own respective channels. I remember an anecdote that was shared on the social media forum Reddit a few years ago that helps illustrate this. A young woman from China came to the United States to study at university. Her roommate, an American, invited the student to come to her family's home for the Thanksgiving holiday. The Chinese student was amazed to see how the American family constantly watched mainstream, cable news programs on the television. The Chinese student earnestly asked her roommate, "Why do your parents watch the propaganda station?" In China, apparently, it is generally understood among the younger generations that the state-sponsored news might not be the most accurate place to hear about what's happening on any given day. Rather, it's understood that a carefully crafted narrative with a particular purpose is aired on those stations. In the United States, we mistake our corporate media for being fair and reliable journalism, instead of recognizing it as a system for advancing the narratives of the ownership class, including those who own and control the mass-media companies.

In China, many young people widely understand that there's no reason to trust narratives that are shared via mass communication from state-owned media. In the US, our younger generations similarly "get it" when it comes to cable-news networks: they realize there's no reason to trust the mass communications we receive from for-profit corporations that are owned by a small number of individuals with private interests, since that ownership class is positioned to benefit from shaping the political landscape of our country. As American thinker and father of modern linguistics Noam Chomsky put it in his famous *Manufacturing Consent*

> The mass media serve as a system for communicating messages and symbols to the general populace. It is their function to amuse, entertain, and inform, and to inculcate individuals with the values, beliefs, and codes of behavior that will integrate them into the institutional structures of the larger society. In a world of concentrated wealth and major conflicts of class interest, to fulfill this role requires systematic propaganda. [10]

An acute and obvious example of this occurred in 2021 when retail investors began buying large amounts of the publicly traded GME (GameStop) stock, causing massive losses for hedge funds who held short positions, betting that the stock's price would fall. Whose side do you think cable news networks supported: the hedge funds or the everyday retail investor? Now, these tactics are no longer limited to our cable news programs. While television and cable news are going by the wayside, companies and organizations have shifted to digital marketing on social media platforms. In 2017, for the first time, the global spend on digital advertising surpassed the global spend on television advertising, and that scale keeps tipping toward the digital world. The dis-informers have found new ways to reach us.

At best, we might understand that these centralized news channels are inherently biased because they are owned by large corporations and need to sell advertising space to survive. Here, Chomsky again reminds us, "Large corporate advertisers on television will rarely sponsor programs that engage in serious criticisms of corporate activities, such as the problem of environmental degradation, the workings of the military-industrial complex, or corporate support of and benefits from Third World tyrannies." In short, it's their business model. At worst, these centralized news stations spread ideological disinformation to meaningfully mislead the public in service of big business, the military-industrial complex, religious and political ideology, and other centralized and organized interests.

In the 2020 court case *McDougal v. Fox News Network, LLC*, Judge Mary Kay Vyskocil determined that any reasonable viewer of the Tucker Carlson Tonight show would approach any statements he makes with an appropriate amount of skepticism. [11]. Even the U.S. courts have determined that our news organizations don't air the news; these are "entertainment" shows that we should approach with healthy skepticism, understanding that the commentators we watch are not stating facts, but mere opinions, often with fabricated information and outright lies.

When we're faced with evaluating the truth of a claim, we can boil down the whole, complex equation to a simple, four-part question: what is the credibility of a source or speaker, what are they trying to make me do or believe, what techniques are they using to make me feel or think that way, and why are they doing it? But no single part of this question is easy to answer. As one team of disinformation researchers wrote in their 2017 study, "Determining who's behind information and whether it's worthy of our trust is more complex than a true/false dichotomy." More than two thousand years ago, Aristotle wrote about *ethos* and the credibility of speakers as far back as 350 BCE. Now, we are just as likely to be fooled by a website, social media post, or vlog as we are to be persuaded by a person physically speaking. But we tend to fall into a default position of trust. If an article, post, speaker, or web page looks vaguely well designed and similar to other things we've read before, we tend to say, "Sure, that looks legitimate! Why not?" without questioning the purpose, intent, or origin of the information.

Credibility is difficult to assess; when we see a well-groomed man in a sharp suit and shiny tie on a cable network—or even in a YouTube video—we are immediately tricked into thinking the person is credible. It's something like the Ted Bundy effect. The infamous serial killer dressed well, spoke intelligently, and carried himself like a well-meaning citizen. In this way, he was able to lure unsuspecting people to horrific deaths at his hands. All the time, we are being tricked in the same fashion. Just because someone is wearing fancy clothes and is sitting in front of a green screen doesn't mean they know what they're talking about. In truth, it doesn't mean anything other than that they purchased a suit, tie, and green screen, and maybe they know how to use some video-editing software. In the same way, we too easily accept the information we read in online spaces to be valid simply because it's there. We think, perhaps even at a subconscious level, "Well, this web page looks legitimate enough. It must be true." But there's nothing qualifying about the existence of a web page in today's day and age. Anyone can create a website with a few dollars and an hour of time. Everywhere around us, we must be more skeptical of the credibility of the information that we see, read, and hear. Too often we see political candidates make speeches on subjects with which they have no formal background. We've never elected a person with a PhD in Environmental Science to the presidency of the United States, yet every candidate for the position speaks confidently and unashamedly about environmental policy as though they are an expert in that field.

When we ask these questions—*what is the credibility of a source? What is it trying to make me do or think? How is it doing that?* and *Why are they doing it?*—we start to engage in a process of rhetorical analysis. That is, we're taking a critical step to stop messages from spellbinding us and working us over, and we start to assess communication in a more objective way. Take a video advertisement for example. We see a Subaru commercial showing a car crash, but then the driver and their child safely walk away, saying they are thankful they bought a Subaru. This is trying to work us over through the method of what Aristotle called *pathos*—an appeal to emotion. The viewer *feels* something: the fear of losing their child, the trauma of an automobile accident, perhaps a lack of safety in their own vehicle. There might be dramatic, cinematic, swelling music that accompanies the advertisement and plays on our nervous system to increase our heart rates and create a sense of uncomfortable tension, which plays even further into this *pathos*. Then, the solution: just buy a Subaru. I have nothing against the Subaru automobile company—I drove an old, green, '98 Subaru Outback for as long as it could possibly last, which

was a long time—but I do have something to say about these tactics and how you can be better prepared to spot them, analyze
them, and not let them influence your life. This is the power of
rhetoric: to ask questions about credibility, intent, and purpose.
The logic of the advertisement is to make you feel fear, and to present you with a solution to that fear: "Buy a Subaru, and all your
problems will go away. Protect your children by buying a Subaru.
Buy, buy, buy. If you don't buy a Subaru, you must not love your
children!" Of course that's their purpose. They're a car manufac-
turer. They're in the business of selling cars by any means necessary. But is it *true*? Will buying a Subaru protect your family better
than their competitor's vehicle? We don't know, and it's too complex of a multi-factorial problem to figure out, even if we had the
best data available. The world's best quantum computer probably
couldn't help you with that one.

So, who is credible? Should we just trust no one? Credibility is
a practical thing to think about. Who are you going to hire to fix
your air conditioner, or perform your spinal surgery? You might
have to look at several sources. You could read a surgeon's biogra-
phy on the hospital's web page, look up their education, and see
where they completed their residency. You could find out where
they got their medical degree and how many years' experience
they have performing the surgery. You can ask that question directly to them: how many times have you performed this operation? You can find public data about the hospital to see what the
post-operation infection rate is, and how it compares to other hospitals. These are all ways of evaluating the credibility of the institution and its messaging. But you must ask those questions: what
is the credibility of a source, what is it trying to make me do or
think, how is it doing that, and why are they doing it? Hopefully
you come to find out that the hospital has a great surgeon who has

years of experience and a great track record that will lead to a positive medical outcome for you. (That was my experience when the brilliant Dr. Craig Coccia performed an L5-S1 microdiscectomy on me when I was still in my twenties.) Skepticism and rhetorical analysis doesn't always mean we have to end up in a place of negativity or conspiracy theorizing. It's really the opposite. It just means we're in search of the truth. We want to find the best solution for our problem.

Yet, we have no perfect institution for discovering truth. Even in the scientific community, for example, data might be faked in a clinical trial to push an Alzheimer's drug to market in the pursuit of profit, or companies like Uber might hire scientists to publish peer-reviewed research that shows their services in a particular light. Human error and greed are everywhere. And, of course, we can hardly trust politicians and public figures who claim to have the benefit of average citizens on their mind while they use their inside knowledge to trade stocks, gerrymander, lie to the public, and block legislation that would help the average citizen with rapidly rising housing prices, stagnant wages, rising consumer debt, outrageously expensive college education, and a host of other real problems that affect hundreds of millions of Americans. Politicians, more generally, seem to just kick the can down the road to the next administration, or even the next generation. We have seen administration after administration promise to fix the housing crisis, the global climate catastrophe, job shortages, infrastructure, and to boost the economy. Yet, the planet's still burning, and people are still homeless and hungry, and it's hard to say anyone's listening to public opinion. Aren't democracies supposed to serve the will of the people? By the people, for the people? If ever there was a group of folks who needed to orient themselves toward truth and read some philosophy, it's the political class.

While our trust in these large institutions like government, news organizations, universities, and science-at-large is diminishing, the average citizen is also being bombarded by increasingly advanced, technologically sophisticated disinformation and misinformation through complex algorithms, digital media, and social media. Despite our general understanding that big-tech companies don't have our best interests at heart, North Americans are still using their smartphones, on average, for more than three hours a day and are exposed to thousands of advertisements every day. Marketers and writers have learned to disguise information as opinion pieces—sometimes called advertorials or referred to more generally as "native advertising"—such that it is becoming harder and harder to determine what is organic, natural content in social media and what is an advertisement. And here's that study again: remember, The Stanford History Education Group found that 96 percent of high school students saw no reason to be suspicious of a web page about global warming "facts" that was published by a fossil fuel company. We tend to assume that anything we read is credible, and we should be doing the opposite. We should be questioning the credibility of everything we read, see, and hear. Just because a web page looks clean and well-designed doesn't mean that it is a vessel of truth and facts. It's easy to build a professional looking website. You can make a whole website in about ten minutes with drag-and-drop web-building tools, which are widely available for anyone to use.

All of this might seem like an insurmountable and world-ending situation. But it may soften your concerns a bit to know that these are problems humans have been dealing with since the dawn of time. That doesn't make our present concerns any less species-threatening, but it does go to show something about the nature of human experience and civilization. It's hard to go anywhere in the world without someone trying to sell you something or lie to your face for their personal gain in the service of their ideology.

The short answer to the question of who to trust is: trust no one but yourself. But if you're going to learn to trust yourself, you must learn to become a better thinker and analyzer of information and credibility. Because if we are so easily persuaded and deceived, how can we even trust ourselves not to be fooled and not to spread misinformation accidentally? Socrates had insight for this, too: we must humbly admit that we know very little about the world and the universe.

## THE ART OF PERSUASION

The best antidote and cleanest answer to all these problems and questions surrounding truth, disinformation, and persuasion are enshrined in the lost, ancient art of rhetoric. Ancient Greeks invented a host of terms and ideas for dealing with problems of credibility and truth. But rhetoric isn't just *how* to persuade; it's also *why* we persuade and the ethics of persuasion. The ancient Greek philosophers were much more concerned about the ethics of persuasion than they were about the technical tricks and artistry of speaking well. I hope to continue this ancient tradition with you in this book. In this ancient sense, rhetoric is not only a toolkit to help average citizens decode and understand the barrage of incoming information and advertisements that they receive in their daily lives, but also a mode of thought and methodology for approaching the world with an understanding of the nuanced and slippery nature of truth, ethics, and human nature. Like I've said before, rhetoric is philosophy with legs. Rhetoric is the great lost art of humanity that is seldom taught in classrooms and receives only passing mention in contemporary discourse. We often hear of rhetoric in a disparaging way, such as in reference to bloviating politicians, but using the term this way obscures rhetoric's fascinating history and the very roots of the discipline.

When rhetoric is done properly, we should want our politicians, journalists, educators, and citizens to be studied rhetoricians. This means that they have read a certain set of texts from classical rhetoric that explore the underlying tensions between truth, reality, and language. To be a rhetorician, properly, is to carry with you a philosophical disposition and skeptical attitude toward information and the way the world works. Rhetoric is a necessary counterpart to science, and a necessary counterpart to living in a complex world with competing meanings and messages. The importance of truth defies political party lines. It doesn't matter if you are a conservative or a progressive. You should care about whether you are speaking the truth, and whether the information you read, see, or hear is accurate.

The ancient Greeks were thinking about the ethics of speech because of the very real social threat that they were observing in their society. Teachers of persuasive speech, the Sophists, were going about as tutors-for-hire, teaching people how to speak well, using rhetorical techniques. The Sophists were teaching people how to be persuasive, but not how to think, nor how to be a good person. In short, the Sophists were criticized for teaching people how to make false arguments and deceive the public. Many works of Plato, especially, are best understood as direct reactions to the Sophists. Granted, not all Sophists were unthinking, unfeeling, evil figures. Not by a longshot. We see a lot of nuance in the works of Gorgias of Leontini, for example, who was one such Sophist and teacher-for-hire. Gorgias seems to have recognized the spellbinding nature of speech and the very real dangers of persuasion, as we see in his extant speech, *The Encomium of Helen.*

So, we have lost an incredibly valuable field of study by dismissing rhetoric as mere trickery and honeyed words. The real goal of rhetoric is to learn to speak the truth. But that is a hard road. It requires looking at issues of truth and credibility and the relationship between communication and our social and civic life. Our contemporary civic discourse does not seem very civil, but it's difficult to determine whether there are any qualities that are particularly alarming. These tensions have always existed. On March 15, 44 BCE, a group of Roman senators stabbed Julius Caesar twenty-three times. Caesar was, more or less, personally responsible for the loss of democracy in ancient Rome, and he did tyrannically take power for himself and away from others, so perhaps it was fitting punishment—it's not my place to say, anyway. The events in Washington, D.C. on January 6, 2021 are on a much smaller scale than the turmoil that ancient Rome faced, but there are, nonetheless, a host of eerie similarities between the decline of the Roman Empire and the present predicaments faced by modern nations such as the United States. The past cannot be used to predict the future, but we can always learn from our mistakes. It is an interesting thought experiment to imagine what Tweets Caesar might have sent during his campaign against Pompey or in the days leading up to his assassination.

Finally, we must come to that burning question: what is truth? How do we know it when we see it? When I told some of my colleagues about my ideas for this book, I got some funny looks and comedic remarks. "A book about truth? Let me know when you figure it out. I've been looking for it."

Everyone has their own theory of what constitutes truth: "Truth only comes from god," or "Truth is socially constructed by multiple individuals who agree something to be true." Yet, these are both flimsy answers. There are too many gods and goddesses to count, every religion puts forward a different version of what is and is not true, and each has just as good a claim as any other. And of course, when it comes to socially constructed theories of truth, it's easy to see that masses of people can be massively misled and propagandized into believing fictions. Millions of people believe the current North Korean leader, Kim Jong-un, has divine powers gifted from God. That doesn't make it true. If a thousand people believe the Earth is flat, that doesn't make it true, even if it is a shared apparent truth between them.

My project here is not to try to tell you what is or is not true (that would be impractical, and I can't follow you around all day to answer your questions), but rather, to help give you the tools to ask the right questions about speakers, videos, advertisements, speeches, blogs, websites, posts, articles, and any text or media that you come across, so that you can better assess its credibility for yourself. Our troubled relationship with truth is not a new phenomenon born of the social-media, "fake-news," digital-disinformation era that we presently find ourselves in. My goal in this book is not to make claims about what the absolute or universal truths of reality are, but to arm you with a set of ideas and strategies for identifying disinformation in your own life so you can better find your own truths and better arm yourself against those who would like to mislead you.

In this sense, I intend this work to be part history, part interdisciplinary synthesis, and part self-help. When we don't know who or what to trust, it can begin to feel like the world is groundless, or like the world we know is falling apart. But if we develop

a strong ability to analyze information—digital or otherwise—
we can start to piece together a cohesive worldview and indepen-
dent sense of self that is less easily influenced by advertisers, big
tech companies, corporations, and political parties. Like many
writers and thinkers, I am still mystified by how someone like
Adolf Hitler could spellbind an entire nation in the early twentieth century, murder millions of people, and nearly cause the col-
lapse of Western civilization. What sort of education or training
could have prevented so many from falling under the spell of his
speeches, radio broadcasts, and propaganda films? And what
new Hitler, for which we are not prepared, lurks in the corner?

## SO, WHAT IS TRUTH?

I must be a good scholar and an honest thinker and tell you that
defining truth is something of an impossible task. The word
means different things to different people at different times. Some
have suggested that truth is just socially constructed—that truth
is whatever two or more people agree it to be. But all you have to
do is imagine yourself stepping into a room full of Flat Earthers
to realize that is not a very good working definition.

There are many different forms of truth. When we look at a
peer-reviewed, scientific study in a reputable journal like *Nature*,
we have an understanding that a rigorous methodology has been
applied and the findings might be replicable. That gets us close to
a kind of scientific truth. But then again, science is always changing and rewriting itself, and you can't always find a peer-reviewed
journal article to help guide you through the decision-making of
daily life. The rigorous and hyper-specific findings of a peer-reviewed scientific article might get you a step closer to solving a

serious problem, but we don't all have the time or discipline-specific knowledge to evaluate these kinds of studies or to apply them to our lives every day. Another conundrum.

Some great philosophers suggested there was no such thing as truth at all. But at the same time, we can't throw away the concept entirely. We need to hold our political representatives and news organizations to certain standards. When we see an advertisement, we expect it not to mislead, nor to misrepresent a product. When we have a conversation with a friend or colleague, we expect to be able to trust what they're saying. The problem is, maybe we shouldn't. We will see how Plato, thousands of years ago in his famous dialogue *Phaedrus*, warned us of those who would falsely persuade us. The ultimate lesson of Plato's *Phaedrus* is his urging that one should first become a philosopher, and *only then* should one be a rhetorician, a speaker. Socrates, speaking in this famous Platonic dialogue, asks the titular Phaedrus: "He then, who being ignorant of the truth aims at appearances, will only attain an art of rhetoric which is ridiculous and is not an art at all?" This is the old maxim to *think before you speak* but on a much higher level. Plato is asking us to engage in the hard work of philosophy, the difficult task of looking beyond the superficial veneer of the world around us. And then, of course, there is the most haunting lesson of all; most people are not philosophers. Most people are not experts in their field. We should not trust most people. People have agendas and interests that cloud their judgment and are aimed at persuading you with false arguments, and they have left their lives and their world unexamined. The world is not black and white. So do not be tricked by those who claim to know the truth before they have considered their subject profoundly, as a philosopher.

What I can say is you should question everything. That's how we're going to get closer to understanding what is true and what is not. For the German philosopher Martin Heidegger, "Questioning builds a way." [12] That's the legacy of Socrates. We must have the humility to realize how little we all know—not just ourselves, but those around us. Wearing a suit and appearing in a YouTube video does not make a person credible. Just because an article was published on a website doesn't mean it was fact checked. It's up to us—every one of us—to assess the credibility of the information we seek out each day. Other people are out to persuade us to buy, vote, think, believe, or change our way of viewing the world. They don't want you to think and ask questions for yourself.

We might not know the truth of everything ourselves, but neither do political candidates, big corporations, or other ideological and religious groups. Don't trust anyone who claims they have all the answers. None of us do.

## Seven Forms of Truth (And Their Limitations)

| Form of Truth | Definition | Limitations |
|---|---|---|
| Scientific Truth | Truth is based on observations about the universe measured through the scientific method. Studies are subjected to peer-review and are replicable. Aristotle first codified this approach. Knowledge comes from observing the world and categorizing, classifying, and taxonomizing it. | Academic standards can vary—see the Sokal Hoax. Can be cost or time prohibitive to replicate studies. Information produced is often hyper-specific and can be difficult to apply to decision-making and everyday life. Many questions cannot be answered with a scientific study: "What should I do with my life?" or "How do we solve the housing crisis?" These are questions that require judgment. |

| | | |
|---|---|---|
| **Religious Truth** | Truth is based on an outside source, such as a god or gods, or truth comes from those who claim to communicate with gods such as spiritual leaders. Or truth is based on texts claimed to be produced by gods or those who have communicated with them. | Impossible to verify evidence for religious claims. Nearly endless competing religious ideas. Religious experiences are subjective and cannot be verified. Authorship of religious texts by divine spirits cannot be proven. No evidence that any humans have ever communicated with divine spirits. |
| **Personal Truth** | Truth is based on personal experience: "Truth is whatever I observe it to be," or "It's my life, so it's my truth to speak." Whatever you believe to be true is true. | Often impossible to provide evidence. Subjective perception of the universe can be inaccurate. Memory can be inaccurate. Most people have ideological biases and deeply held values which distort their perception of the world. |
| **Postmodern Truth** | Truth is socially constructed, or truth is whatever multiple people agree that it is. Truth is not something discovered, but something invented by humans. | Groups of people can share inaccurate or false perceptions of reality, such as in Germany in the 1930s, or the "Flat Earth" community. If anything can be true, then nothing is true. |
| **Absolute Truth** | Truth is based on universal properties that can be discovered through reason, logic, philosophy, or other forms of intellectual discovery. Plato's theory of Ideal Forms is an example of this model of truth. | Anthropocentricism. Limits of human perception and reason. Varying and irreconcilable accounts of the universe that are not always replicable. |
| **Practical or Folk Truth** | Truth is based on one's localized learning from whatever they've happened to stumble upon in their schooling, work experience, community, or local network. | Folk logic can lead to superstition and an unexamined life. What is true in one's own community might not be true outside of that community. |
| **Rhetorical Truth** | What seems to be true can actively change based on the best available information. Truth claims are evaluated by the credibility of the source or the speaker and examined for the validity of their argument. | Endlessly recursive investigations into a subject eventually exhaust resources, such as time or limits of human knowledge. Access to information may be limited, or one may not have skills to interpret sources from outside one's own field. |

RHETORIC IS A MODE OF ALTERING REALITY...

—LLOYD BITZER [13]

# CHAPTER II

# The Persuadables

*Every audience at any moment is capable
of being changed in some way by speech.*
—LLOYD BITZER [14]

## FOR THE LOVE OF SPEECH

The ancient Greeks loved speeches. In the beginning of *Phaedrus,*
one of my favorite dialogues by Plato, the titular character
Phaedrus tells Socrates that he has just returned from a morning
of making speeches with his friend Lysias. This would seem to be
a rather funny thing in today's world: to meet a friend for lunch,
ask them how they spent their morning, and be told, "Oh, I was
just over at Jane's apartment. We were making speeches all morning." Though this would not be a common occurrence today, the
art of making speeches was close to the heart of ancient Greek
culture. In a world where writing was a relatively new technology, writing tools and materials were expensive, and there was a
reliance on oral tradition. Thus, speechmaking was a valued pas-
time. In many ways, this same desire for communication and

storytelling is now fed by our media addictions: television, You-Tube, film, podcasts, or binging a Netflix series. We don't want to dismiss the important differences in our cultures, but we also shouldn't forget just how similar humans can be across time and space.

But rhetoric wasn't all fun, games, and entertainment for the ancient Greeks. The renowned classicist and scholar of rhetoric, George Kennedy, explains in his seminal *A New History of Classical Rhetoric* that this fascination with speeches was at least partially due to the vital, life-saving necessity of wielding language persuasively. Because there was no regular system of legal representation in ancient Greece, citizens would often be required to defend themselves in a court of law or to lay out their case against an opponent.

In these early days of democratic society, your ability to speak could literally be a matter of life or death. If your neighbor accused you of stealing their goat—or worse, their horse—then you better have been able to make a compelling argument about why it wasn't possible that you stole it as you proved your innocence. Perhaps you would make an appeal to *ethos*—that is, your character and credibility—and say, "I am an honest and law-abiding citizen of Athens. How could a person like me commit such a crime?" Perhaps you would make an appeal to *pathos*—that is, the emotions of your listeners—by pleading, "I am a father of five children and must work hard to provide for them. Would you rob these children of their father by imprisoning me based on the false claims of this greedy accuser?" Or perhaps you would appeal to the *logos* (or logic) of the audience and claim, "I was all day yesterday at the Theatre of Dionysus, a fact to which many of my fellow citizens can attest. How could I have been in two places at once?"

Today, we don't take language seriously enough. The rhetorician Lloyd Bitzer wrote in his oft-cited essay (and bane of disinterested undergraduate students everywhere) "The Rhetorical Situation" that "rhetoric is a mode of altering reality," not by physically moving material objects around, but by "the creation of discourse which changes reality through the mediation of thought and action." This is just an academic way of saying that speech and language can literally change the way we perceive the world, the way we think, and the way we act. And certainly, we know this to be the case. We might hear a powerful sermon and be swayed into a life of service to a god, or we might see a compelling video advertisement which, even imperceptibly or insensibly, cements an idea in our mind of which make and model of automobile we want to purchase. Language can have life-altering effects on us. We may be convinced to take a job in a new city or to vote for a particular political candidate. Gorgias, the rockstar rhetorician of ancient Greece, likened language to a kind of drug, or *pharmakon*. To me, that appears to be a reasonable explanation for the brainwashing and spellbinding experienced by the German population under Hitler in the early-to-mid twentieth century. But then, it's easy to see when it's happening to other people: "How could all those Germans have just fallen right in line with that evil man? Couldn't they see through his lies?" No, most could not. It's easy to see when others are being persuaded. It's painful and difficult to observe it in ourselves. We like to believe we are immune to persuasion, but we are all persuadable.

It's not just language that is persuasive, though. It is the combined effects of rhetoric that persuade us. Hitler's powers of persuasion included his mannerisms, gesticulations, the timbre and inflection of his voice, his word choice (*diction*), the way he constructed sentences (*syntax*), and his use of rhetorical techniques like *allusion* or *antithesis*. It was his use of symbolism and architecture (such as the golden eagle, standard in the grand Nazi-party rallies and the ubiquitous swastika) as well as his deft wielding of then-new technologies such as radio, film, and fast travel by airplane. As Quintilian told us, even "the mere look of a man can be persuasive." Contemporary psychology tells us just as much. Tall people make more money over their lifetime, according to findings on a "height-salary link" that was documented in one study by Timothy A. Judge, PhD and Daniel M. Cable, PhD.[15] In another uncomfortable set of studies, researchers found that attractive women received higher grades in college courses—an effect that diminishes when teaching is conducted remotely and online.[16] We like to think that we're objective, rationale, and fair, but there's a broad expanse of research that shows the opposite to be true; we're easily persuaded and carry many deeply held biases and values within us, and these affect the way we perceive and interact with others and the world around us.

We don't understand, fully, comprehensively, scientifically, *how* persuasion works. There is, at present, no satisfactory or complete picture of persuasion in the neurological, psychological, rhetorical, or sociological literature. It's a tricky beast to pin down precisely. Persuasion is complicated. We are practically left with the same conundrum today as our ancestors faced thousands of years ago. In some sense, I am grateful for this. I have no doubt that if a universal theory of persuasion were discovered, corporations, political parties, and governments would take full advantage of the knowledge, and democracy would be in further jeopardy. Yet, even without a universal theory of persuasion, this is essentially the place we find ourselves in. Using imagery, video, hyper-targeted social media advertisements, psychographic profiling techniques, big data, modern computing power, and complex technological distribution mechanisms, persuasion and propaganda have become more powerful and more dangerous today than ever before. As I will write about later in this book, the UK firm Cambridge Analytica used weaponized social media advertising strategies to influence elections all over the world, while companies at present are spending more money on digital advertising than print, billboards, mailers, leaflets, radio, television, magazine, newspaper, and all other forms of traditional advertising combined. And they called those they targeted with the bulk of their budget "The Persuadables." The Persuadables were a demographic of centrists Cambridge Analytica profiled as being on-the-fence and able to be pushed to vote for one candidate over another. While we don't know the extent to which Cambridge Analytica influenced presidential election results in the U.S. in 2016, we can rightly assume that companies wouldn't be paying for such services if they didn't yield results. Digital disinformation is a massive global undertaking, and we are the targets.

Now, I'm not suggesting that we return to the oral culture of the ancient Greeks and all start making speeches as a form of entertainment. (It might be fun, though.) We can't force a cultural change like that. But what should be most shocking to us is that we have completely abandoned the one field of study that deals directly with disinformation, propaganda, and information literacy in this time of crisis, when there is more technologically advanced disinformation threatening democracy than ever before in the history of humanity. The field of study that deals with these extraordinary questions of truth, credibility, disinformation, propaganda, and information literacy is the study of rhetoric. I know that teaching and learning about rhetoric can be interesting (and even fun) when done right. Furthermore, there may not be anything more powerful for a person to learn than how to speak and write effectively and persuasively. How can we live in a time like this and not teach our children about rhetoric, the field of study that could empower them to disarm disinformation, advocate for their rights and values in an increasingly polarized realm of political discourse, and be resilient to the thousands of advertisements and propagandic messages that are launched at them daily from smart phones, computer screens, and the increasing number of screens in our homes, schools, and places of work? How else to protect them from the idealogues that fill our schools, companies, and communities? Rhetoric is that secret, ancient discipline that can help us in our great time of need. We are all *persuadables*, and we need help.

## WHY WE LIE AND THE BIOLOGICAL BASIS OF RHETORIC

Are humans alone in their lying and deception? Certainly not. It's not unique to our species at all. That revered and aforementioned classicist and rhetorical scholar George A. Kennedy writes in his *Comparative Rhetoric* that humans are not the only deceitful creatures on our planet: "Animals engage in deceit all the time, as when they hide under a bush awaiting prey. Some birds give calls that seem to be intended to deceive other birds" and "an ape may pretend to see or hear something that is not there to mislead others for its own advantage." [17] Kennedy tells us about a chimp named Matata who "would send a trainer out of the room on an errand, then grab something from another animal and yell and scream as though she were being attacked. When the trainer rushed back she should look at him with a pleading expression and make threatening sounds at the other animals." We're the human animal, after all, and when it comes to survival, morality and law can go out the window. Consider the case of Jean Valjean from Victor Hugo's literary masterpiece, *Les Misérables*. If you have no other option, you might also steal some bread to feed your hungry children. We all probably would.

We are moved to action by our emotions, desires, and needs. We are biological creatures with bodies in the world. We get hungry, thirsty, cold, and tired. We have a need to conserve our energy and to survive. In his *Comparative Rhetoric*, Kennedy makes a compelling case that rhetoric is essentially a "form of mental and emotional energy" in light of an opportunity that "may be affected by utterance." [18] The origin of rhetoric—of persuasive communication—is self-preservation, which aligns with rhetoric's history in ancient Greece. In *A New History of Classical Rhetoric*, Kennedy describes ancient Athenian citizens' need to defend themselves in front of a court of law—a life or death situation—which necessitated persuasive speech. Likewise, we can see the serious urgency of communication in the non-human natural world where warnings, mating calls, and cries for help are widely observed across species. Humans are not the only creatures who persuade and who lie.

But can this theory of Kennedy's be applied in the digital, technological age we find ourselves in? In modern capitalism, a company's survival and growth is its greatest priority. The company, party, or organization will do whatever it must to sustain itself, even if that means deceiving or violently attacking an opponent or competitor. This is not at all unlike the instinct of a goat to ram a rival male with its horns, or a gorilla deceiving its troop so it can solitarily sneak off and snack on the tastiest fruits without the notice of others. If the fate of a fossil fuel company is at stake, it will lie to you about human-driven climate change.

They'll lie straight through their teeth, all day long, until the cows come home.

We're not all such bad folk though. Most people don't lie. A 2021 study by Tony Docan-Morgan, Professor of Communications at the University of Wisconsin – La Crosse, found that the majority of self-reported lies were committed by only a few individuals. About 75 percent of the survey participants lied very little or told small, white lies—the kinds of harmless deception that we deal out in interpersonal communication, like telling a partner that "Dinner was great!" when it wasn't particularly delicious, because you want to communicate your appreciation more than anything else. Granted, you still need to be careful with white lies. They can snowball out of control, and before you know it, you'll be eating under-seasoned frozen chicken breasts for the rest of your life. But jokes aside, three-quarters majority of the survey respondents lied zero-to-two times per day. The top 1 percent of liars, however, averaged seventeen lies per day. That's a lot of lies. It's difficult for me to imagine how stressful my life would be with that many lies to keep track of, and how disconnected from reality and compassion for others my life would be if I lied so frequently. But, interestingly, the study's most salient feature was its longitudinal nature—this was one of the first ever long-term studies of lying. Dr. Docan-Morgan found that the amount that one lies varies significantly from day-to-day.

From reading of this study and placing it in the context of my own knowledge of human communication and rhetoric, it seems to me that lying requires two essential factors. The first is the person must have a particular disposition or character that permits lying as a communicative possibility. Most people deliberately choose not to lie. Now, the reason or capacity for this is not a fully sketched -out phenomenon. We learn to tell the truth as a value, which we glean from stories, parents, teachers, and social systems. For ancient Greek thinkers like Plato, there was the *daemon,* a guiding voice like our modern conception of the conscience. For Plato, this *daemon* was not unlike the modern cartoonish representation of a devil and angel sitting on each shoulder, guiding (or goading) us toward a particular action; in fact, Plato considered the *daemon* to be a kind of intermediary between our world and the world of the gods.

The second factor to produce a lie is that conditions must arise wherein the person finds it advantageous to lie—the lying (if not manifested of a recognized mental illness or product of a delusion) is a response to a particular situation. Here is where Kennedy comes into play again—he demonstrates that lying can be advantageous to our survival or to getting what we want. Lying is a rhetorical response, not just to a communicative situation, but to the various pressures and conditions of reality—like a fossil fuel company whose survival depends upon convincing millions of people that the science surrounding climate change is incorrect.

And this is only a simple explanation of the survival instinct. The backdoor channels through which money moves to support various political or ideological positions is incredibly complicated, obscured, and hidden in elaborate schemes of deception.

## THE FUNCTION OF DECEPTION BEYOND SELF-ENRICHMENT

But the purpose of deception is not limited to personal gain. We must lie to ourselves to make sense of the horrifying positions we find ourselves in as humans. It's not easy being an animal on a rock hurling through space, trying to make sense of a noisy, busy world with so many competing interests, fast-paced deadlines, obliga-tions, and so on and so on. But lying is not just something children do when they want to get their way. Kids' lies might seem more obvious to us because we know they are absolutely false. We might ask a five-year-old, "Did you eat the rest of the cookies from the plate in the kitchen?" And through a mouthful of crumbs, they'll say "No, it wasn't me." We ask them, then, "Oh, it sounds like you're eating something. What are you eating right now?" and they say, "Nothing." There's a kind of humor to this sort of lie, because it is so blatant and obvious. We think we can spot a lie like this everywhere. But it's harder to know when something is a lie when it is carefully crafted and persuasively sold to us.

We give too much credence to stories and allow ourselves to be worked over by lies when we *want* to believe them, such as when some politician claims to value the working and middle class, while doing little-to-nothing to try to better the quality of life for everyday citizens. Not long ago, a German WWI veteran persuaded millions of Germans to build hundreds of work and death camps to enslave, torture, and murder millions of Jewish, Roma, Sinti, Black, and gay people. The narrative that Hitler sold to the German people was that Jewish people were responsible for the country's downfall—it was a vague, difficult-to-prove po-sition that vilified an entire group of people. It was perfect pro-paganda to motivate a country to commit horrendous atrocities.

Propaganda works that way; if we don't stop to think critical-ly about propaganda, then what's been said can, on the surface, seem to make a lot of sense. Consider slogans like "Save the Plan-et!" or "Support Our Troops!" It's hard for either a liberal or conservative to take an opposing view to either of those positions. Propaganda works across party lines. "What, you don't want to save our planet? How could you not want to save our planet?" Or

"What do you mean you don't support our troops? They're putting their lives in danger every day for our freedom!" These are effective propaganda slogans because they can be used for almost anything. We can ask people to "Support Our Troops" for either a just or an unjust war. We can ask people to "Save the Planet" in promoting a bill that would have no tangible benefit to slowing global warming. These types of propaganda slogans stir our emotions and get us excited, but they are worse than meaningless because they cloud our judgment and can stop us from analyzing the positions, proposals, and policies that lie beneath them.

Aristotle, the ancient Greek philosopher who was also a student of Plato's, can help us unravel slogan-based propaganda statements. The underlying logic of these propaganda slogans is fairly simple. When a politician flies the banner of "Support Our Troops," our minds naturally fill in the rest of the logic. The syllogism looks something like this:

A: People should always do what is right.
B: Supporting our troops is the right thing to do.
C: Therefore, I should support our troops.

Honestly, it's hard to argue with that logic. But when we break down the actual policies underneath these types of slogans, we can start to see where we err in our thinking. The proposition B is where the politician is attempting to persuade us. It's very hard to argue against proposition A in this syllogism: "People should always do what is right." There are some outlying circumstances, perhaps, and we could open that up to an interesting dialogue. But it's proposition B that is troubling, because B is so vague and nearly meaningless. What does "support" even mean? And which troops? Should we "support" the soldier who commits war crimes and murders civilians? Most of us would not support these actions. Should we support the invasion of another country, unquestioningly, just because of the logic of this syllogism? That's what those in power would like you to do.

If we reconfigure the syllogism from the perspective of the speaker/politician, we get closer to the truth of what is happening. Let's imagine they were speaking honestly to us:

A: I believe invading Afghanistan is the right decision to make.

B: We should always support our troops.

C: If you support our troops, then you should support the invasion of Afghanistan.

We have translated the nonsensical logic of what the politician is saying into a more honest statement. When we lay it out like this, it makes no sense to us: "There are complicated reasons for staging an invasion into another country. I want support from the public for many complicated reasons, too, including for my re-election next term. Rather than tell you about the debatable, contestable, complicated factors that are involved in this problem, I am shifting the focus away from the policy and onto the soldiers. So, support our troops, even if my policies and decisions are wrong!" And if political leaders were truly honest, they would tell us about their investments into the military-industrial complex and tell us about the personal, financial gains they might receive through a military conflict.

Bad logic and bad reasoning accounts for many of our belief systems. It's incredibly unfortunate, because in our complicated social and economic systems, we need to outsource tasks and specialize: we need some people to focus entirely on being excellent medical providers, to keep up with the latest medical literature, conduct research, and help keep us healthy. We need other people, who have backgrounds steeped in physics and engineering, to specialize in designing bridges. We need still other people who specialize in the construction of those bridges. You wouldn't want the architect holding the welding torch, and you wouldn't want the welder in charge of securing financing for the project. That's specialization.

Through this system of distributed specializations, we are forced to place our trust in others—that's hard to do, since we so often misplace our trust. Yet, the very basis of complex social, economic, and governmental systems resides in our ability to trust others. Unfortunately, our trust is often poorly placed. Noam Chomsky tells us of the role of propaganda in the United States in the 1930s after the passing of the Wagner Act, a major legislative victory that gave workers the right to organize. Chomsky writes that in that decade, big businesses relied heavily on public-relations strategies to attempt to curtail the progress of labor organizers, including concerted action by the National Association of Manufacturers and the Business Roundtable:

"The first trial was one year later, in 1937. There was a major strike, the Steel strike in western Pennsylvania at Johnstown. Business tried out a new technique of labor destruction, which worked very well. Not through goon squads and breaking knees. That wasn't working very well anymore, but through the more subtle and effective means of propaganda. The idea was to figure out ways to turn the public against the strikers, to present the strikers as disruptive, harmful to the public and against the common interests...." [19]

The propaganda message that the corporate interests came up with was about harmony and Americanism. They tried to paint the strikers as being disruptive and breaking the harmony and union of American patriotism. "We should all try to work together, we shouldn't be striking!" was the basic idea. It's hard to fight against propaganda like that. Who wants to be considered anti-American? The message was effective and public perception started to change against the strikers. As Chomsky writes, "It was later called the 'Mohawk Valley formula' and applied over and over again to break strikes. They were called 'scientific methods of strike breaking,' and worked very effectively by mobilizing community opinion in favor of vapid, empty concepts like Americanism." The more abstract the messaging, the more powerful it can be, when it comes to propaganda. It's hard to argue against abstract values like justice and patriotism.

We've seen a similar phenomenon in the spread of COVID-19 anti-vaccination misinformation. Despite the vaccine being demonstrably safe and incredibly effective at slowing the spread of coronavirus transmission, mis-and disinformation surrounding the vaccine was quickly and widely disseminated on social media. In May of 2020, NPR reported that researchers at Carnegie Mellon University had found that 45 percent of the Twitter accounts spreading disinformation were automated bots, rather than actual human users of Twitter: "Researchers culled through more than 200 million tweets discussing the virus since January and found that about 45 percent were sent by accounts that behave more like computerized robots than humans. It is too early to say conclusively which individuals or groups are behind the bot accounts, but researchers said the tweets appeared aimed at sowing division in America." [20] In an interview with NPR, Carnegie Mellon computer science professor Kathleen Carley suggested that "We do know that it looks like it's a propaganda machine, and it definitely matches the Russian and Chinese playbooks, but it would take a tremendous amount of resources to substantiate that." It's hard to combat disinformation when it's being spread by non-human actors at great speeds, replicating like a virus itself.

In Aleksandr Dugin's Russian ideographical manual, *The Foundations of Geopolitics: The Geopolitical Future of Russia*, he suggests that Russia's strategy against the United States should be to sow disorder and confusion and fuel instability. The book has been used as a training manual and ideological grounding point for Russian leaders since its publication in 1997. Dugin writes that Russia should "introduce geopolitical disorder into internal American activity, encouraging all kinds of separatism and ethnic, social, and racial conflicts, actively supporting all dissident movements – extremist, racist, and sectarian groups, thus destabilizing internal political processes in the U.S. It would also make sense simultaneously to support isolationist tendencies in American politics" and to promote "Afro-American racists." [21] Any of this sound familiar?

When we return to thinking about George Kennedy's rendering of rhetoric as a natural method of self-preservation—a sort of biological, communicative impulse—then we can see why such a seemingly nefarious global policy would make sense. In fact, American propaganda is some of the most entrenched and effective propaganda in the world. Chomsky writes, "Usually the population is pacifist, just like they were during the First World War. The public sees no reason to get involved in foreign adventures, killing, and torture. So you have to whip them up." [22]

And that's precisely what United States leaders did to promote American involvement in the First World War in Europe and to engineer public opinion to support their policy. Though it's an overly simplistic analogy, in this Kennedyian communication-as-biological-conservation-of-energy interpretation, a country is somewhat like an animal. The leaders of a country make a decision the public does not support. They are in power, and believe they have made the best decision, despite the complete lack of public support. So, those in power use communication technologies and strategies to change public opinion. Time and again, it works. Whether it is propaganda to stoke patriotic fervor in support of a war, or a foreign government sowing division with disinformation, we are incredibly susceptible to lies, and we are easily persuaded. The animals in power want to stay in power. The country in power wants to stay in power. Self-preservation. And so, people will lie to get what they want.

But here is the rub: We can clearly see this is not democratic. This is not rule of the people, by the people, and for the people. This is the elite and powerful influencing the masses. And in order to combat this phenomenon, we must become aware of how these systems are affecting us now, not just through old, traditional media like radio and television but also through social media and new means and methods of transmitting information. A government that persuades its citizens to vote a particular way is not a democratic government. An economy in which billions of dollars are spent lying and persuading its consumers is not a free market. And a school system that does not teach students about these dangers is not providing our children and future citizens a proper education. We should value the truth above all else, if only for the reason that it will create a stronger, more honest democracy, and democracy might be the one thing on Earth truly worth fighting for.

So, don't let yourself be one of the persuadables. Fortify yourself against lies and deception. Be critical. Ask questions such as, *should I trust this article? What are the credentials of this blog's author? Who targeted me with this video advertisement, and why did they do it? Who paid for this political advertisement to appear in my feed? Does this person have the requisite education or training to be speaking on this topic with such confidence? What is the substance of their arguments?* These are tough questions, and you won't always have the answers. But it's better to ask these questions, to consider these elements of persuasion, than to be misled and misdirected by the persuasive powers of others. It's an age-old lesson: Think for yourself.

After all, Abraham Lincoln warned us of the dangers that can crop up inside our own nations. Sometimes we have more to fear from ourselves. In his speech "The Perpetuation of Our Political Institutions," Lincoln gave an address at to the Young Men's Lyceum of Springfield, Illinois, on January 27, 1838:

"At what point shall we expect the approach of danger? By what means shall we fortify against it?—Shall we expect some transatlantic military giant, to step the Ocean, and crush us at a blow? Never!—All the armies of Europe, Asia, and Africa combined, with all the treasure of the earth (our own excepted) in their military chest; with a Buonaparte for a commander, could not by force, take a drink from the Ohio, or make a track on the Blue Ridge, in a trial of a thousand years. At what point then is the approach of danger to be expected? I answer, if it ever reach us, it must spring up amongst us. It cannot come from abroad. If destruction be our lot, we must ourselves be its author and finisher. As a nation of freemen, we must live through all time, or die by suicide." [23]

Today, we may have other threats than ourselves. But in a politically polarized nation, the danger feels close. Think for yourself, and you might be able to help in bringing a critical, civil discourse to our world.

## Evaluating a Source to Avoid Dis/Misinformation

| | Might Be a Credible Source | Need to Do More Research | Beware: Might Be Disinformation | Danger: Likely Disinformation |
|---|---|---|---|---|
| Targeting of the Information: How did you come across this information? | The information or source was not targeted to you based on your demographics or online behavior. you actively sought out the source in your research and took the time to evaluate and investigate the source, the publisher, the author, and the credibility of the source. The information is peer-reviewed and of high quality, and is cited by others in a scientific context. This is the best way to avoid dis/misinformation. | The information was recommended to you by a person you believe you can trust, such as a teacher or experienced colleague. You should still take the time to look up the information yourself and see if it has been relayed to you accurately, and attempt to evaluate the information yourself. Dis/misinformation can still spread this way, and people often confidently talk about subjects outside of their area of expertise. | The information was recommended to you by someone who is not an expert on the subject, such as a friend or family member. you should be very cautious, and not conflate the trust of personal friendship with expertise in a subject. You should look up the source/information yourself and evaluate it. This is how dis/misinformation easily spreads. | The source was targeted to you in the form of a sponsored post or advertisement, such as in a social media feed or as a video advertisement on a platform like YouTube. You did not actively seek out the source—someone targeted you with this information. Though it may not be clear exactly how, the advertiser has targeted you based on your online behavior, interests, or demographics. |

| Credibility of an Author/ Speaker/ Other Media: What is the *ethos* or credibility of the author or information? | The author is an expert in their field, or the study is conducted by multiple authors who are experts. You have "triangulated" sources by looking at other studies or reviews to see how other experts have responded to the original source. The source is cited by other experts in the field, and you have examined the various arguments for/ against their perspective. | The author or speaker is an expert in their field but is speaking about a different topic than their field of study. You should still research the credibility of the author, speaker, or media object. It is easy to be fooled by people who claim to be experts or who make themselves appear to be experts. Even experts can often speak on subjects outside of their area of expertise when they have no special knowledge of that field. | The author or speaker is not an expert in their field, but may have some practical knowledge of the field or some years of experience that they are relying on. They are not necessarily a bad source but may not have the highest caliber of information on the subject available. You should still conduct your own research on the topic. | The author of the information is a company, corporation, political organization, or other entity that has a particular interest in persuading me to do something, buy something, or think a particular way. This source has no expertise on the subject on which they are speaking or may even have a conflict of interest. This is almost always a form of obvious persuasion and could be disinformation. |
|---|---|---|---|---|
| Purpose of the Source: Why was the source created? What was the intent? | The article, book, video, or other source was created to share new knowledge. It was published in a reputable, peer-reviewed academic journal or by an academic or credible publisher. The source was created in an academic, scholarly context with a clear methodology. | The source was published in an academic or scholarly context, but it may be outdated, or new information may be more relevant or accurate. You should still seek out more information to check against this and "triangulate" this source in the context of other information. | The purpose of the source is not clear. Perhaps it is native advertising, such as an informational post about a subject on a blog or a well-researched video or vlog. You should seek out better information, but you might use this source as a starting point for the beginning of your research if the author is credible and cites reliable sources. | The article, web page, social media post, video, or other media object was created with a specific call to action in mind. It was intended to make you think a certain way, persuade you of something, or make you buy something or click on something. This was created to persuade you, and you should not trust it. |

| Style of the Source: How is the source presented and what are its biases? | The source provides data, analysis, and conclusions in a neutral and objective tone. The source provides a clear methodology of how the data was obtained. The source is aware of its own limitations and does not try to extrapolate beyond its scope. Even disinformation can look scientific in its style, so you should still be careful to evaluate other elements of the source, such as its author, the reputation of the publisher, and you should check other sources to gain context. Disinformation can sometimes look like a reputable web page or scientific study, so you still must be careful. | The source provides data, analysis, and conclusions in a mostly neutral tone, but there appears to be a bias or other prejudice in the presentation of the material. You should do more research on the credibility of the author and their background and explore other sources to contextualize the information. Perhaps the information is outdated or otherwise not as timely and up to date as it could be. You should seek a wider context for the source and evaluate its arguments. | The tone is not neutral, and the speaker, author, website, or other source seems to have a particular set of values or belief system and an obvious bias. The source may not explicitly ask you to do something or vote a particular way, but the bias permeates the source and is evidently a persuasive piece. You should assess the claims that are being made and find better sources so you can examine the data and primary sources yourself, instead of listening to someone else's interpretation of them. | The source is inflammatory, excessively emotional, or designed in such a way as to play on your values or emotions. Emotional manipulation can be subtle, such as a video with the use of dramatic or cinematic music or an emotionally invested speaker. The source does not have a neutral or objective style. It is asking you to believe something, think a certain way, or act a certain way, perhaps even in a threatening or fear-inducing manner. This is clearly designed to persuade and disinform. |

...THERE IS NO GENUINE ART OF SPEAKING WITHOUT
A GRASP OF TRUTH, AND THERE NEVER WILL BE.

—PLATO [24]

## CHAPTER III

# Enchanting the Mind

*And when the orator instead of putting an ass in the place of a horse puts good for evil, being himself as ignorant of their true nature as the city on which he imposes is ignorant; and having studied the notions of the multitude, falsely persuades them not about 'the shadow of an ass,' which he confounds with a horse, but about good which he confounds with evil. What will be the harvest which rhetoric will be likely to gather after the sowing of that seed?*

—PLATO [25]

## THE BROAD-HEADED ONE

How do we tell fact from fiction? How do we know when we're being taken for a ride by a friend, public figure, politician, or various media? It may come as some surprise that these are not entirely new problems. Fake news, disinformation, misinformation, dishonest leaders, and propaganda are decisively *old* phenomena that humans have been dealing with for thousands of years. We've established that well by now. Humans have a long history of searching for truth through science and philosophy, and just as long of a history of telling great lies to one other for personal gain. To help guide us in how we might deal with these issues today, we can look back to the past to see how our first philosophers dealt with truth and deception.

One of the most significant and lesser-known texts to which we can turn is the dialogue *Phaedrus* by the ancient Greek philosopher Plato, which will take center stage in this chapter. *Phaedrus* is one of Plato's literary and philosophical masterpieces, where he explores issues like the nature of rhetoric, the limitations of writing as a technology, the ethics of speech, and the divine gift of madness. It's a wild ride and not an easy read, but is deeply consequential and rewarding. The conclusion that Plato ultimately reaches in *Phaedrus* is of extreme importance to us; he says there should be no art of using language without philosophy. That is, a speaker must care about the truth and seek for the truth *before* they speak or write about a subject. Otherwise, they are no real rhetorician at all. They are just a Sophist: a trickster who is a weaver of lies and deceit.

The human tendency to lie and evade the truth served as direct inspiration for some of our most important thinkers in the ancient world. If we want to discover truth, after all, we will have to contend with the people who do not take it seriously. If we want to know the truth, we'll have to pick it apart from the lies. Spiritual truths are claimed in many ancient texts as far back as the "Kesh Temple Hymn" inscribed on an ancient Sumerian tablet, dating to 2600 BCE, which was about 4,600 years ago. We also have extant religious texts from the world's first named author, the High Priestess Enheduanna, born in 2268 BCE, which we will visit in a later chapter. Interestingly enough, humans have long granted gods and goddesses the power of deceit, too. In

Hesiod's writings, dated approximately to the seventh or eight century BCE, we see the appearance of Apate, the goddess of deceit, and her male counterpart Dolos, the spirit of trickery.[26]

Plato is dealing with a different kind of truth in his work. He is primarily interested in his Ideal Forms, which constitute a kind of absolute truth. He believed that everything in our world was a shadowy representation of an ideal form. That chair you're sitting in? It's not a perfect chair, but a representation of what the perfect chair could be. One of the easiest ways to get a grasp on Plato's theory of these Ideal Forms is to imagine a circle. Let's say you get some technical drawing equipment like a compass, and you draw a circle on a piece of paper. It looks really good. It looks like a circle. You measure it, and it measures—as well as you can tell—like a perfect circle. But then, what would happen if we took a microscope to it? We would see imperfections. We would see the texture of the paper and where it's caused the pen or pencil lines to be jagged. It's never going to be absolutely, perfectly circular down to the smallest level. Yet, we can *imagine* a perfect circle in our mind. The idea of a perfect circle exists in the universe, but it can never manifest itself in physical reality. That perfect circle, the idea of it, is an Ideal Form.

Plato wanted us to be big thinkers. He was tired of Sophists going around ancient Athens teaching people how to be great speakers without first being great thinkers. The Sophists were savvy tutors, and they earned decent money selling their teaching services to the wealthy and elite. The Sophists could use tricks of speech, body, and voice to make "the lesser causes seem the greater." In short, they could teach you how to persuade. Thus was born the early art of rhetoric. Our ancient wise Greeks understood the power of language and its ability to shape our perceptions of reality. It's no coincidence that the ancient Greeks took these topics seriously; they really are serious business. Plato wrote about many topics, of course, but rhetoric was a subject he returned to frequently, as did many other ancient thinkers.

You can undoubtedly think of countless applications for effective speech in contemporary society as well, from acing a job interview to making your intentions known to a potential romantic partner. We are constantly using language to impress, persuade, and influence. That usage carries a lot of responsibility. Yet, there is something empty and problematic about effective speech for the mere sake of effective speech, isn't there? There were no *ethics* to the Sophists' approach, Plato realized. The Sophists taught only the technical and artistic skills related to speaking well. To put it bluntly, Plato did not like the Sophists. His dialogue *Gorgias* is an outright attack on the Sophists and the so-called art of rhetoric. It is in this dialogue that the word *rhetorike* (rhetoric) makes its first appearance in humanity's extant written history. Plato's thinking regarding *rhetorike* shows more subtlety in the dialogue *Phaedrus,* where things get a bit more complex. Nonetheless, it is not entirely wrong to say that in the vacuum created by the Sophists, philosophy was born. Plato understood that a bunch of people going around speaking well about things they knew nothing about was a recipe for disaster. In this way, the origins of the entire Western intellectual tradition can be seen as a reaction against the Sophist tricksters of language.

But who was this man, Plato, and why should we care? Plato was a student of the most famous of philosophers, Socrates. Socrates left no written works behind. For many classicists and scholars, Socrates, Plato, and Aristotle form the basis of Western intellectual thought. As Alfred North Whitehead famously remarked, "The safest general characterization of the European philosophical tradition is that it consists of a series of footnotes to Plato. I do not mean the systematic scheme of thought which scholars have doubtfully extracted from his writings. I allude to the wealth of general ideas scattered through them." It's a big claim, and probably not entirely accurate, but it helps to show the enormity of Plato's influence on today's world. There were many pre-Socratic philosophers who also deserve credit, and it's clear that humans were asking questions about our origins, creation, and the universe, far before Plato. [27] But with Plato we have, really, the first philosopher whose rich diversity of ideas survive across multiple extant texts, and the first person to ask profound questions about our individual, psychological lives. These questions have resonated for generations across cultures, languages, and time, and include: What does it mean to live a good life? Why are we here, and what should we be doing with ourselves? and How should we structure our societies?

And it was from Socrates that Plato learned to think this way. Socrates was one of the first thinkers who dared to wonder how the world might be different, and how we might be different in the world. Socrates was courageous enough to question the established orders of society and imagine alternate realities. In some ways, that's the dream of progress we are still carrying forward today. We are still asking, how might my life be better, and how might I help make the world slightly better during my blipof existence on this rocky little planet? But Socrates left no writings behind, so we have Plato to thank for writing Socrates as a character in his dialogues and presenting us such a rich diversity of early ideas that still echo through time.

There are a few stories about how Plato got his name. It seems it was a nickname that caught on. Seneca tells us the following about Plato: "His very name was given him because of his broad chest." And Diogenes goes further to suggest the nickname stuck for three reasons: because of the breadth of his physical size, because of his intellect and eloquence, and because of his large forehead. *Platon* means broad. Broad, too, were Plato's intellectual interests. His dialogues set the groundwork for many of our academic disciplines, including psychology, philosophy, ethics, and rhetoric. Still, why should we care now about some broad-foreheaded wrestler from Athens who wrote dialogues more than two thousand years ago? My students are frequently unafraid to ask that question, and it's something I'm glad for, because it is true to the Socratic spirit of questioning everything and questioning authority. It's not unusual for me to hear something in the classroom or in an online discussion board "when I teach virtually" along the lines of *what is the point of reading this stuff?* Or, *Where is this going?* Fair enough. Keep reading. It takes a moment to unpack. But it's a rewarding journey. In fact, from my students' very earnest questions came the inspiration for this book. By the end of the semester, my rhetoric students are often amazed and troubled by this long-lasting human struggle for truth. And I suspect you will be, too, since you're still here reading.

One contemporary textbook succinctly summarizes the relationship between truth and rhetoric in this way:

Some of the earliest rhetoricians argued about the nature of truth and how it related to rhetoric and discourse. Plato disliked rhetoric and the Sophists because of their relative relationships to truth and lampooned them in his writing. In some ways, this debate never truly left us, and has resurfaced with renewed fervor in contemporary times. Beginning with Friedrich Nietzsche who wrote that there was no truth as early as the nineteenth century, ideas about truth and its relationship to rhetoric have been at the heart of changing rhetorical theory." [28]

This is not only the "debate that never left us" but also one of the most destabilizing problems of the twenty-first century. But none of this is cut and dry. These are complex issues, and they were complicated for our ancient friends as well. To better understand how Socrates and Plato attempted to deal with issues related to truth, we will have to look more directly at their lives and writing.

## SOCRATES THE STONE-CUTTER

Only one of the many books I own directly mentions Socrates's profession prior to his becoming the philosopher we know him as today. I find this a bit curious. It seems that, as a young boy, Socrates learned stone cutting from his father who'd worked on the famous Parthenon. Socrates himself may have carved a handful of fairly famous statues, and there is a line in the *Republic* that supports this, or is perhaps the origin of this story. "You are a sculptor, Socrates, and have made statues of our governors faultless in beauty." [29] It's not hard to imagine some nice metaphor to go along with this: carving ideas from the conversations he had with others, striking and hammering away with his words to see what beautiful things lie beneath. This is essentially the Socratic method: ask lots of questions until no more questions can be asked. Cut away all the nonsense until you get at the heart of it, until you reveal the kernel or the truth. Children are especially good at this. You will quickly find out how little you understand about the way the world works when you're asked, "Why is the sky blue?" followed by "But where did the sun come from, then?" It gets tricky fast. There is a sweet kind of grace in these interactions; there's the opportunity to express the virtue of humility in acknowledging what we do not know. Better yet, questions are an opportunity to learn more about these things ourselves and share that process of discovery with the children in our lives.

One striking similarity between us and our ancient thinkers and rhetoricians is the turmoil that we are living through. They found themselves in a search for truth parallel to what we find ourselves in. So, too, were there parallels in the bloody conflicts and political disruptions of the ancient world. History repeats itself, as they say. Right in the middle of Socrates's life, in 431 BCE, the Peloponnesian War broke out between Athens and Sparta. Athens had begun its democratic project less than a hundred years earlier and was finding prosperity as a seagoing, mercantile city of a few hundred-thousand people.[30] Citizens were generally happy with their newfound liberty and the discovery of a government that they could participate in and build themselves. These were good times. So good, in fact, that they were the conditions under which the foundations of today's intellectual thought developed. But not everyone was having a good time. There were some thirty thousand eligible male voters. Women and slaves could not vote. It's harrowing and worth thinking about that it would take over two thousand additional years for us to collectively wake up and adopt the Nineteenth Amendment to the US Constitution, giving women the right to vote, and that it was not until 1964 that the Civil Rights Act was brought to life. (Though Black Americans were supposed to have been given the right to vote in 1870, this right was systemically infringed upon, and still is.)[31]

We still owe some debt of gratitude to the ancient Athenians for imagining a system of participatory government and enacting it. But this new democracy was threatened by their Spartan neighbors, a more warlike people with profoundly different values. Strict and hardened warriors, the Spartans had little interest in luxury, wealth, fine arts, and the natural philosophy that the Athenians were so carefully cultivating. A dispute over who would control western sea routes to Sicily and South Italy—particularly routes that brought grain and metals to the growing civilizations—led to a tiresome series of bloody engagements that stretched both Athens and Sparta to their limits. [32] It's not hard to imagine that amid the chaos and uncertainty brought by twenty-seven years of constant warfare, certain thinkers turned inward, asking themselves essential questions about the nature of human morality and what makes a person virtuous. In some sense, the Peloponnesian Wars were as much a conflict about values—liberal, democratic Athens against aristocratic, warlike Sparta—as it was about trade routes. [33] These conflicts were the birthing ground of thinkers like Socrates and Plato, among many others.

This brings us far enough to start discussing what I consider to be Plato's master work, the inexhaustible *Phaedrus*. To understand how these Platonic dialogues work, we can easily think of a contemporary podcast where two or more people have a lengthy, spirited, and generally good-natured conversation about a set of related, complex topics. This seems to be the correct way to understand the dialogues, really. The central art form of discussion and dialogue has survived through humanity's many technological revolutions. Plato seems to have thought that through the dialogic process, we can arrive at some truth. Aristotle would later build on this and show that, in fact, dialogic processes demonstrate what we do not know. Neither position is exactly correct. But again, we might think of these dialogues almost like fictional, creatively written podcast scripts of the past. They are meant to imitate the actual conversations that Socrates would have had with citizens of Athens, but they are also used to illustrate Plato's thinking.

You'll find that the dialogues are curious texts. Plato's dialogues are not precise treatises about exact topics. They flow and meander. Some of them are even very funny, such as the introduction to *Gorgias* where Callicles suggests, "The wise man, as the proverb says, is late for a fray but not for a feast." It's important when reading the classical texts to try to find a bit of humor and lightness in them. Our ancient friends were good jokers, after all, as evidenced by the many comedies of the age. Remember, too, that a large amount of vulgar graffiti was discovered at Pompeii—this gives us a sense of how our humor has not changed much over the ages. At times, Plato's dialogues go into very silly territory, such as with the opening of the dialogue *Protagoras*, where Socrates cannot help but comment on Alcibiades's fresh and handsome beard, a potentially romantic advance. [34] As I say, when reading Plato, it helps to find some of the lightness, bounciness, and passion that's in the text.

One of the most salient light-bulb-moment insights that I share with my undergraduate students is: "Don't be afraid of these old philosophers. They were wrong about a lot of things, and right about some things, and we're still trying to figure it out. When we read these old texts, we try to take an objective, neutral position, and understand them in their historical, cultural, and intellectual context. We neither want to dogmatically praise them, nor dogmatically, critically bash them so hard into the ground that we miss their significance." In fact, taking either of these positions is the mistake I see students make most when they approach ancient texts. It's the same mistake people make when they approach any literary, classical, or even scientific work. If we start off too critically and come out swinging, believing, "these old, dead philosophers can't teach me anything!" then that's going to become a self-fulfilling prophecy; they really won't teach you anything if you don't let them. You lock them out by doing this and commit an *ad hominem* logical fallacy in the process. But in the same vein, when we approach Socrates, Plato, Aristotle, or any of the others with too much sacred reverence, we miss the opportunity to critique and question them and may even miss some of the subtlety of their thinking. Try to approach with an open mind.

And there is no doubt, again, that our ancient friends were absolutely, horribly wrong about a lot of things. Aristotle very stupidly wrote that "small people can never be beautiful," and of course it's obvious in our modern views that the practice of pederasty now seems creepy and predatory, or worse. Perhaps the best way to approach these old books is with the notion of the Burkean Parlor in mind. When we read these authors, we are trying to have a conversation with them and their ideas. The rhetorician Kenneth Burke, from whom this idea of the Burkan Parlor is named, put it like this:

> "Imagine that you enter a parlor. You come late. When you arrive, others have long preceded you, and they are engaged in a heated discussion, a discussion too heated for them to pause and tell you exactly what it is about. In fact, the discussion had already begun long before any of them got there so that no one present is qualified to re-trace for you all the steps that had gone before. You listen for a while until you decide that you have caught the

tenor of the argument; then you put in your oar. Someone answers; you answer him; another comes to your defense; another aligns himself against you, to either the embarrassment or gratification of your opponent, depending upon the quality of your ally's assistance. However, the discussion is interminable. The hour grows late, you must depart. And you do depart, with the discussion still vigorously in progress." [35, 36]

We Americans don't have a good sense of what a parlor is, so I add that you can just as easily imagine a bar or a coffee shop. When you read and write about Plato, you can picture him sitting there at your local pub, and he's been there for a while. He's had a few drinks and is waving his arms around a bit as he makes his points. We grab a drink and sit, and we listen and offer him the respect we offer any decent person. But then, we must realize we can jump in and contribute to the conversation as well. We are allowed to talk to Plato. His perspective is not gospel. And for that matter, even Biblical gospel is not Gospel, as it is just one more "hot take" on reality, albeit one of the more profound and long-surviving sets of apparent truths that haunt and inform us. But what about truth and language?

## DIVING INTO PHAEDRUS

Alright, you've filled up your mug of coffee or tea, you've sat down in the parlor, and you're still with me. *Phaedrus* is an exceptional dialogue in that it so carefully renders its setting and its place. It gives us a lot to work with in terms of imagining the life of ancient Athenians and in particular, Socrates. We learn through this dialogue that Socrates considers himself, not a man who is interested in nature, but one who is at home within the walls of Athens. Socrates tells us he is "a lover of knowledge, and the men who dwell in the city are my teachers, and not the trees or the country." It's again worth pointing out, though, that we should remember Socrates is just a character in Plato's dialogues, and we do not know the extent to which Socrates may or may not have said the same things of himself, though Plato is likely one of the best sources on his master. Still, I think we may understand Plato to be writing his Socrates a bit tongue-in-cheek in these lines. Socrates learns from his fellow city dwellers by questioning them, prodding them, and poking them with his incessant questions, irritating so many people that he was eventually tried by the court of Athens and sentenced to death. *Phaedrus* would have been written about thirty years after Socrates was sentenced to death, something that Plato never quite forgave the citizens of Athens for doing.

Figure 3: Henry Bacon, *General View of the Acropolis at Sunset*

Few of the Platonic dialogues are so beautifully situated in a place as *Phaedrus*. We have Socrates actually leaving the walls of the city of Athens in this dialogue. And it's hard, at first, to imagine why Socrates would be so reluctant to explore the pastoral countryside around Athens until we remember some of our earlier context. With the constant warfare between Athens and Sparta, and the potential confrontations with any number of small tribes and factions that might be roaming the countryside or settled in pockets, we can start to understand why a person would prefer to stay safely enclosed within the fortifications of a city like Athens. Athens must have felt like such a haven to so many people—not just Socrates. It was a shining light of democracy, culture, wealth, and trade, and stood in opposition to the confusing, brutal, violent world outside the walls. Most of us don't live in walled cities today, but it was the norm for thousands of years. A city needed walls to keep out invaders, raiders, and any number of other threats. That all became obsolete when heavy cannons were invented and the walls of Constantinople came crashing down in 1453. But that's a fabulous story for another time.

Before they even enter any philosophical or significant discussion of the major themes of the *Phaedrus*, our two characters, Socrates and Phaedrus, basically spend their time conversing on where they would like to sit down to do their speech-making. Remember: ancient Athenians loved getting together to share speeches. Phaedrus has just come from listening to speeches with his friend Lysias. As we've earlier discussed, in ancient Greece, speech-making was a regular event of good fun and entertainment. This was also how Sophists would attract their students and make money, by delivering spectacular speeches to great crowds in the streets. It is a great intellectual exercise to practice making speeches on extemporaneous themes in front of others. Ancient Greeks found a lot of pleasure and amusement in doing this, and this practice sharpened their speaking skills for their professions and civic life, while also sharpening their thinking. When we put our thoughts on the line in spoken form, we feel an added seriousness, danger, and urgency. We know when we are wrong when we say something out into the open air and it sounds wrong. Our consciences are at least that good. Try telling a lie out into the open air: it should be uncomfortable, it should hurt a little. We see later in the dialogue how this affects Socrates through his conscience, his *daemon*.

Here we can reproduce part of Benjamin Jowett's translation of these opening sequences of the dialogue to show the great care which Phaedrus and Socrates take in picking out a spot to sit and talk:

> **Socrates:** Lead on, and look out for a place in which we can sit down.
> **Phaedrus:** Do you see the tallest plane-tree in the distance?
> **Socrates:** Yes.
> **Phaedrus:** There are shade and gentle breezes, and grass on which we may either sit or lie down.
> **Socrates:** Move forward.
> **Phaedrus:** I should like to know, Socrates, whether the place is not somewhere here at which Boreas is said to have carried off Orithyia from the banks of the Ilissus?
> **Socrates:** Such is the tradition.
> **Phaedrus:** And is this the exact spot? The little stream is delightfully clear and bright; I can fancy that there might be maidens playing near.
> **Socrates:** I believe that the spot is not exactly here, but about a quarter of a mile lower down, where you cross

to the temple of Artemis, and there is, I think, some sort of an altar of Boreas at the place.

**Phaedrus:** I have never noticed it; but I beseech you to tell me, Socrates, do you believe this tale?

**Socrates:** The wise are doubtful, and I should not be singular if, like them, I too doubted. I might have a rational explanation that Orithyia was playing with Pharmacia, when a northern gust carried her over the neighboring rocks; and this being the manner of her death, she was said to have been carried away by Boreas. There is a discrepancy, however, about the locality; according to another version of the story she was taken from Areopagus, and not from this place. Now I quite acknowledge that these allegories are very nice, but he is not to be envied who has to invent them; much labor and ingenuity will be required of him; and when he has once begun, he must go on and rehabilitate Hippocentaurs and chimeras dire. Gorgons and winged steeds flow in apace, and numberless other inconceivable and portentous natures. And if he is skeptical about them, and would fain reduce them one after another to the rules of probability, this sort of crude philosophy will take up a great deal of time. Now I have no leisure for such enquiries; shall I tell you why? I must first know myself, as the Delphian inscription says; to be curious about that which is not my concern, while I am still in ignorance of my own self, would be ridiculous. And therefore I bid farewell to all this; the common opinion is enough for me. For, as I was saying, I want to know not about this, but about myself: am I a monster more complicated and swollen with passion than the serpent Typho, or a creature of a gentler and simpler sort, to whom Nature has given a diviner and lowlier destiny? But let me ask you, friend: have we not reached the plane-tree to which you were conducting us?

**Phaedrus:** Yes, this is the tree.

**Socrates:** By Here, a fair resting-place, full of summer sounds and scents. Here is this lofty and spreading plane-tree, and the agnus cast us high and clustering, in the fullest blossom and the greatest fragrance; and the stream which flows beneath the plane-tree is deliciously cold to the feet. Judging from the ornaments and images, this must be a spot sacred to Achelous and the Nymphs. How delightful is the breeze:-so very sweet; and there is a sound in the air shrill and summerlike which makes answer to the chorus of the cicadae. But the greatest charm of all is the grass, like a pillow gently sloping to the head. My dear Phaedrus, you have been an admirable guide. [37]

Now, this is usually where I would stop if I were in a classroom with my undergraduates and I would say something like, "You just read some Plato. And it wasn't that bad after all, was it?" You can see now that there's really no reason to have any anxiety about digging into these ancient texts. They are quite comprehensible if we are patient with them, and they are much richer than we generally imagine. So rich, in fact, that they may offer guidance to us still to this day in these difficult issues of disinformation and truth. That's why we're here. But it will take some more time to walk through the context of the dialogue to get to the bigger ideas about rhetoric.

In these opening remarks of the dialogue, we get the first hint of the major theme of the power of speech. Socrates says something like, "Yet you seem to have discovered a drug for getting me out (*dokei moi tes emes exodou to pharmakon heurekenai*). A hungry animal can be driven by dangling a carrot or a bit of greenstuff in front of it; similarly if you proffer me speeches bound in books (*en bibliois*) I don't doubt you can cart me all around Attica, and anywhere else you please."

What an idea, that speech can be like a drug! But is this not the case? I don't think it is hyperbole to say that speech may be like a drug, and it's a theme we see in many ancient Greek texts, so much so that it may have been, more or less, a universally held belief that speech could spellbind us. We see, now, how thousands of years ago, our ancient philosophers were beginning to tease out the extraordinary effects that language can have over us. But this is just the start of the dialogue and the beginning of the unraveling of the theme.

Allow me now to just generally discuss the structure of the entire dialogue, whether you intend to read it in its entirety or not. I do suggest you go read it, at some point; it's widely available and you can find the classic Benjamin Jowett translation (and others) floating around on the Internet.[38] For all the disruptions and dangers of the Internet, there's a lot of good that can still be done with it and a lot of good that's still happening. I still hold out hope for a technologically driven New Renaissance. It was those who escaped from the sack of Constantinople with copies of ancient Greek works in the 1400s who would go on to birth the Renaissance, in turn so connected to the Scientific Revolution. And, well, here we are today. In a very real sense, we can thank the ancient Greeks for our computers and modern technologies. Without the revival of interest in ancient Greek thinkers, there would be no Renaissance. No Renaissance, no Enlightenment. No Enlightenment, no Scientific Revolution. No Scientific Revolution, no Industrial Revolution. See where I'm going? Of course, it's reductive, but it's nice to wrap our heads around big-picture history sometimes. You're more connected to Plato than you realize.

Regarding *Phaedrus*: it is structured into two main parts, which we'll simply call the first half and the second half of the dialogue. The first half of the dialogue features these discussions of settings and place and finding a nice spot underneath a tree. It then features three speeches. The first speech in the dialogue is delivered by Phaedrus, and he is reading a scroll from Lysias. The speech is about love and how we shouldn't take someone to be our lover who is truly in love with us, because they are mad or insane. Socrates then gives a speech on the same topic as Phaedrus, but tries to do it better, desiring to show off his artfulness as a speaker. Then, Socrates delivers a second speech after his first. That's the whole first half of the dialogue. The second half of the dialogue deals with more back-and-forth banter between Socrates and Phaedrus about the relationship between rhetoric and philosophy, and finally ends with a fantastic section about writing as a technology and the Myth of Theuth. Not too bad, right? First half: three speeches. Second half: rhetoric and philosophy and writing as a technology. You've got this.

Back to the beginning. This first speech that Phaedrus reads from the scroll that he had tucked up in his sleeve, a speech originally delivered by his friend Lysias, is Plato craftily giving us an example of what he thinks is a bad speech. This is, in part, why you can't just read the first few pages of the dialogue—all you will get is a bad speech! You must eventually read the whole thing. In this first speech, the arguments are poorly formed. It is rambling and incoherent. There is little artistry in the speech. And the central argument of the speech is baffling even to a modern reader's common sense: that a person should reject the advances of those who love him and should instead accept the advances of a non-lover. Granted, there are many ways to be married and be in love, and not all of them must be based on a romantic, passionate love. Many marriages work well when they are based on practical, material, or financial arrangements; perhaps Lysias was onto something, and we can certainly have an interesting discussion about the merits of Lysias's arguments. But for many modern readers, the ideas that Lysias wrote in his speech conflict with ingrained American values about the very idea of what love should be and what love really is. And this was as apparent to Plato's character of Socrates as it is to us now, though they are talking more about pederastic relationships, a topic I'm not exactly going to be unpacking in this chapter, for want of space and time. In short, wealthy adult men in ancient Greece commonly took on young men in a sort of complex mentor/mentee relationship that was sometimes romantic and sometimes sexual. It is important context for the dialogue because there is an apparent love interest between Socrates and Phaedrus, the two main characters, and we can sometimes read into the dialogue a kind of flirtatiousness between them.

Socrates, in the dialogue, hears this speech delivered by Phaedrus and congratulates him on the oration. Socrates flatters him, but then the two begin ribbing and teasing each other. The truth comes out. It was a bad speech. Phaedrus challenges Socrates to deliver a speech better than the one written by Lysias. Socrates asserts that Phaedrus has been caught up in the rhetorical force of the speech. Socrates eventually gives into this playful banter and decides to give a speech of his own. But he is embarrassed to do this, because he knows that to deliver a more artful speech on this same theme and with this same central argument would be dishonest. Thus, he hides his head while he makes his speech (the second speech of the dialogue). Now, we should stop at this juncture to realize how significant this is. Socrates agrees to invent a properly constructed argument to demonstrate to Phaedrus how an artful speech should be made. But he can hardly bring himself to do so. He is ashamed of making a false case with fancy language. This is the kind of rhetoric that our ancient philosophers were rallying against, the rhetoric of the Sophists, the kinds of people who make beautiful arguments simply for their magic, whether in the service of good or evil. There is a magic and a power in language that we still, with contemporary neuroscience, language theory, and robots on Mars, do not fully understand—in fact, we hardly understand it at all. But Socrates is willing to perform it, here, just to show Phaedrus that it can be done. A bad argument can be made to sound artful and entirely convincing.

We'll stop here, just to take pause and note: look how many interesting topics we've already covered, and we haven't even broken into the most famous and interesting parts of the dialogue. This goes to show just how sweeping and rich the Platonic dialogues can be. I think if there is a "right" way to read Plato, it is to consider these dialogues as springboards for further investigation and conversation. Scholars will always argue about what precisely Plato meant by this or that line—the line numbers are called Stephannus numbers, by the way—but the true value of Plato is the wealth and breadth of ideas that he brings forward to us to this day. Not least of which is this important investigation into the interwoven relationship between the power of language and how we use language to represent truths about reality.

In Villa ab Academia attributa
Sua Plato condit Academiam
Salvator Rosa Inv

*Figure 4: 17th Century depiction of Plato in the Garden of his Academy*
*(Plato at Center)*

...WON'T SOMEONE WHO IS TO SPEAK WELL AND
NOBLY HAVE IN MIND THE TRUTH ABOUT THE
SUBJECT HE IS GOING TO DISCUSS?

—PLATO [39]

## CHAPTER IV

# Plato's *Phaedrus*

*But could it be, my friend, that we have mocked the art of speaking more rudely than it deserves? For it might perhaps reply, 'What bizarre nonsense! Look, I am not forcing anyone to learn how to make speeches without knowing the truth; on the contrary, my advice, for what it is worth, is to take me up only after mastering the truth. But I do make this boast: even someone who knows the truth couldn't produce conviction on the basis of a systematic art without me.*

—PLATO [40]

## THE BREAKING POINT

The great aim of Plato's *Phaedrus* is to show us that one must first be a philosopher before one is a rhetorician. There is a great danger in a powerful speaker who is thoughtless. You can imagine Mussolini or Hitler very easily as examples. Plato was reacting against the rhetorical teachers-for-hire of his day, the Sophists, who Plato thought were unethical in their approach. Plato accused the Sophists of being tricksters, teaching Athenians—citizens of

Athens—how to craft persuasive arguments without ever teaching anyone how to *think*. It's a valuable lesson that we need now, more than ever. How many times have you seen a person confidently talking about a subject which they have little to no expertise in? This is how misinformation and disinformation spreads; a person speaks, writes, or otherwise communicates across media without seriously considering their subject. Afterall, disinformation is the intentional spreading of untrue information. Misinformation is the accidental spreading of untrue information. And how can we know what is true? For Plato, at least, the way to discover truth is to be a philosopher. The philosopher is someone who stops and considers their subject with depth and complexity and doesn't just go around making claims about things they know nothing about. First, one should be a philosopher, and only then should one be a rhetorician. This is Plato's salient argument that grows through the dialogue, and it's why *Phaedrus* is so powerful.

We'll pick up again where we left off with *Phaedrus*. We'll talk about Socrates's second speech, now, in which he flips the arguments of the first two speeches upside down. Socrates's con- science—his *daemon*—is bothering him because he cannot truth- fully say that madness is wholly evil, that we should not take a lover who is madly in love. He finds this to be blasphemous. Madness is a great gift from the gods, Socrates will tell us. Then, after Socrates provides these proofs of divine madness, he gives us his famous Allegory of the Chariot, where he likens the soul to a chariot being pulled through the heavens by a good and bad horse. It's riveting stuff. Finally, in the second half of the dialogue, Socra- tes works out a theory of rhetoric—that it is a way of directing the soul by means of speech, and that a rhetorician must first be a philosopher so that he understands the nature of the soul and the truth about the subject upon which he is speaking. This sounds dense, but there is practical wisdom in it; before we speak or write upon a subject, we ought to try to ascertain some truth about that subject. Those who do not research, consider, and philosophize about the subjects on which they speak are mere tricksters—and this is precisely how disinformation and misinformation is formed and spread throughout societies.

Back to *Phaedrus*: Something extraordinary happens after Socrates's first speech. Socrates begins working himself up into a fine, almost musical frenzy of excitement. We know that a great speaker can become carried away with their own words, caught up in the moment, seemingly carried along by some divine inspiration. It is not unlike a great musician who is improvising. This is often described, in contemporary terminology, as a state of *flow*.[41] And that is a useful framework in which to consider it. However, Plato thinks of this quite differently; there is something more, almost a sense of possession, of indescribable divine inspiration. Indeed, the very etymology of *inspiration* seems to suggest *breath*, as if the gods themselves were breathing into us. Robert Cavalier of Carnegie Mellon University reads this section of the dialogue, at the end of the second speech (Socrates's first speech) as follows:

> "Socrates breaks the speech at this point, as if waking from a trance. He comments about how he feels in an inspired state of mind and of how the place seems filled with a divine presence. The reference is to the strangeness of this spot by the river Illius and, in this context, it points directly back to the invocation of the Muses at the beginning of the speech. *It is as if Socrates has been carried away by the mythic surroundings of his discourse and is in fact singing a song that he has no control over. He states specifically that he is caught by the nymphs and almost uttering dithyrambs.*"[42]

Interestingly, in contemporary computer science, a daemon is a computer program that runs in the background without direct involvement or input from the user. This is far away from what Plato would have meant by his inclusion of a *daemon*, here, but it's not too far away from the truth. For ancient Greeks, the *daimon/daemon* was a lesser god, a guiding spirit. Homer used the term *daemon* and *theos* almost interchangeably in mentioning the gods, though there is a much more specific meaning that is evident in the dialogue *Phaedrus*. We see Socrates nearly leave the scene of this speech-making. He is done with making speeches, he is ready to return to the city, he has had enough of it! He physically can't stand to make speeches with untrue arguments. He is going to cross the river and head back to town when something powerful grips him. It is his *daemon*.

This *daemon*, this inner, guiding voice that was so powerful in Socrates—yet seems to be missing from many of our contemporaries, whether politicians, business leaders, the ultra-wealthy, or neighbors, sisters, and brothers—calls him back to tell the truth about the matters at hand. His conscience is speaking to him. Socrates knows that this speech he just made—though it was artful, well-constructed, and even rhetorically and poetically inspired in places—did not get to the heart of the issue. It was not true. It was not right. And his *deamon* has guided him to this realization like a kind of inner light, an intuition presented as an inkling sensation that there was something more to explore. A sense that the truth was not yet uncovered.

This brings us to the third overall speech of the dialogue, or what we can also simply call Socrates's second speech. Here is where things get particularly interesting because this is where we get a clearer glimpse at Plato's thinking and an elaboration of some serious themes. In this second speech by Socrates, we see the theme of love and madness emerge. Socrates begins his second speech with the following construction, showing us how madness is actually a gift from the gods, and effectively overturning the arguments of the first two speeches of the dialogue:

> **Socrates:** Know then, fair youth, that the former discourse was the word of Phaedrus, the son of Vain Man, who dwells in the city of Myrrhina (Myrrhinusius). And this which I am about to utter is the recantation of Stesichorus the son of Godly Man (Euphemus), who comes from the town of Desire (Himera), and is to the following effect: "I told a lie when I said" that the beloved ought to accept the non-lover when he might have the lover, because the one is sane, and the other mad. It might be so if madness were simply an evil; but there is also a madness which is a divine gift, and the source of the chiefest blessings granted to men. For prophecy is a madness, and the prophetess at Delphi and the priestesses at Dodona when out of their senses have conferred great benefits on Hellas, both in public and private life, but when in their senses few or none. And I might also tell you how the Sibyl and other inspired persons have given to many an one many an intimation of the future which has saved them from falling. But it would be tedious to speak of what every one knows. [43]

Magic words, drugged-like states of mind, and madness as a gift from the gods... Are these the sorts of things we should be teaching our students about, Dr. Lawrence? Well, yes, absolutely. I joke a bit, here, but these are significant ideas with which to contend, not unlike how Shakespeare's *Hamlet* features ghosts, betrayal, indecision, and murder, or how our religious and mythological stories are rife with monsters, battles, and mayhem. Being a human is not an easy thing, and it gets quite messy sometimes. Plato is weaving a web of complex ideas for us to consider. What Socrates is telling us is that madness is divine, madness is a gift. And not just for prophecy, but he goes on to say that madness can be a gift from the Muses which inspires our lyrical and artistic creations. While we understand this relationship between mental illness and creativity a bit more thoroughly in contemporary psychology, it still holds great mysteries. Where do the ideas for a song, a book, or a speech come from? What breathed so much fire and spirit into Mozart, and was it from within or without? Even as I write these words on the page in front of me, there seems to be no coherent explanation for the complexity of the process—which does not mean it may not be fully explained in scientific terms one day. That's not what I mean to say. Rather, the relationship is more complicated than simply saying, "I decided to write a song, so I thought of the notes in my head, and then I picked up my instrument and played the song." One almost needs to be struck with the idea, and one must be a little bit mad to push the boundaries of human artistry and experience to do something novel, unique, and interesting in artistic and creative spaces. They say that riots broke out after Stravinsky debuted "The Rite of Spring" in Paris in 1913, though there is sufficient academic debate about the reasons. Like any subject—I don't pretend to be a scholar of Stravinsky. That's a matter of ethos, or credibility, and it is something we'll discuss later at great length. *Who should we trust and why* are matters of credibility, or in Aristotle's terminology, *ethos*." [44]

Socrates then breaks off, a bit recklessly but powerfully, from his questionable proof of the immortality of the soul, which is riddled with bizarre axioms and faulty logic, but may have made good sense to ancient readers. It is after Socrates breaks off from this section that we have one of the real jewels of the *Phaedrus*, which is Plato's famous Allegory of the Chariot. Plato has Socrates describe the human soul as being like a chariot, pulled by two horses, and soaring through the heavens. There is a good horse and a bad horse. The gods, by comparison, have perfect chariots with whole teams of good horses. The best horses for the gods, of course. But we mere mortals are always being pulled in opposing directions. And is this not a fit metaphor for the internal struggles we face? In American cartoons and animation we often see this represented with the figure of a devil on one shoulder and the angel on another, debating about the right course of action. Should I order the pizza, or should I eat something healthier? What's the worst that could happen if I run to the liquor store for some more whiskey? This push and pull is constantly working its way out in our innermost beings day in and day out.

If we allow our bad horse to take over, so to speak, we will be pulled down to earth and live a life of over-indulgence, vice, and mundane horrors. If we allow our good horse to lead us, we will continue upward past the heavens to the places only gods can go, and we will see the colorless, shapeless place of true knowledge. Plato, I think, is being quite sincere in playing out this metaphor. He has Socrates tell us, "the reason why the souls exhibit this exceeding eagerness to behold the plain of truth is that pasturage is found there, which is suited to the highest part of the soul." Here, Plato tells us he is referring to the souls of philosophers, artists, and those of a musical and loving nature. This is interesting because we find many other places in ancient Greek thought where music and musicians are not cast in such a favorable light, but that is a topic for another place." [45]

In our own studies, we are approaching the real meat of the matter, and so we should go back to the primary source.

(**Socrates:**) ...Thus far I have been speaking of the fourth and last kind of madness, which is imputed to him who, when he sees the beauty of earth, is transported with the recollection of the true beauty; he would like to fly away, but he cannot; he is like a bird fluttering and looking upward and careless of the world below; and he is therefore thought to be mad. And I have shown this of all inspirations to be the noblest and highest and the offspring of the highest to him who has or shares in it, and that he who loves the beautiful is called a lover because he partakes of it. For, as has been already said, every soul of man has in the way of nature beheld true being; this was the condition of her passing into the form of man. But all souls do not easily recall the things of the other world; they may have seen them for a short time only, or they may have been unfortunate in their earthly lot, and, having had their hearts turned to unrighteousness through some corrupting influence, they may have lost the memory of the holy things which once they saw. Few only retain an adequate remembrance of them; and they, when they behold here any image of that other world, are rapt in amazement; but they are ignorant of what this rapture means, because they do not clearly perceive. For there is no light of justice or temperance or any of the higher ideas which are precious to souls in the earthly copies of them: they are seen through a glass dimly; and there are few who, going to the images, behold in them the realities, and these only with difficulty. [46]

With my students, I tell them that while there is no trophy or medal at the end of the course, they do at least get to say that they have read some Plato when they have finished the semester, and they can talk to their friends and family about ancient Greek philosophy somewhat intelligently, and that's quite a nice reward in itself. They are, perhaps, a bit shaken by all of it. In American high schools, we adopt a kind of reverence, perhaps, towards great authors like Hemingway or Fitzgerald, only to later learn they were roaring drunks or worse. But those are *ad hominem* arguments—an unfair attack against the life and humanity of the person, not their ideas. The stories of these lives cannot diminish the thinking or artistry they accomplished. Hell, according to Plato, half the time, it is the madness that made them so great. If we want to be good scholars, we should take our *ad hominem* fallacies seriously. But admittedly, I am not always strictly scholarly in my own mind, and I sometimes dream deeply about the lives of the figures we are taught to revere, and of course, I question the canon, like so many of us do. Why is it Plato that we are still reading, of all people? Perhaps you are starting to see why. My point here, is that you can at least pat yourself on the back at having cracked open some of ancient Greece as you read these passages. They don't need to be phantasms in the back of your mind any longer. You can sit down next to Socrates and Plato in the Burkean parlor and have a bit of a chat with these figures. You can play their thoughts around in your mind.

Importantly, here we see Socrates being a practitioner of his own theories. Socrates was unwilling to speak falsely on a subject. He does not want to be a mere Sophist, a trickster of language, an empty rhetorician. Socrates wants to show us that he is a true philosopher, someone who considers his subject deeply. He pokes a giant hole in the speech written by Lysias. What if madness is not a curse, after all? What if madness is a great gift? It's not the validity of the argument that is interesting to us, now—obviously gods and goddesses aren't going around literally gifting humans with mental illness; that's a strange delusion. But Socrates's philosophical approach is a model for us. He is unafraid to pry, prod, and flip an entire issue upside down. This is what we must do as proper rhetoricians and honest philosophers. We must ask the big questions; we must turn arguments upside down and inside out to get at the truth.

Consider the question, "You say that you are the best candidate for the presidency because you will make the country great again. But what do you mean precisely by 'great'?" It's still undefined. That's why it's such effective propaganda; it's loose, nebulous, and un-philosophized.

## THE MIND ENCHANTED

Socrates continues forward with his speech from this point with a discussion of goodness and badness, and I must truncate my writing a bit here to get to more pressing matters. We have now essentially finished the first half of the dialogue. The first half of *Phaedrus* is concerned with these themes of love, madness, speech, and the soul. The second half of *Phaedrus* deals more explicitly with rhetoric and the nature of speech. Rhetoric, or what it has evolved into over the millennia, can be summarized basically as the art of effective communication. But this is a stripped-back, watered-down definition. For Plato, rhetoric had to be paired with philosophy for it to be a real art. Rhetoric is mere flattery and trickery if the speaker does not first think profoundly about his subject. Rhetoric and philosophy must be paired together. And as I've written many times, we see what happens when people become powerfully persuasive without philosophy, a sense of ethics, and a questioning mind; with that dangerous combination, we produce some of the worst villains of human history.

Rhetorical scholars mostly teach writing classes, which are important parts of high school and university curriculum in the United States, although it's not clear that rhetoric is being taught effectively when the Stanford History Education Group has documented that 96 percent of students in one study did not detect a conflict of interest in a web page about global warming published by a fossil fuel company. Rhetoric is both a toolkit for analyzing information (such as in this example, a good rhetorician would know to question the *ethos* of the web page, for *ethos* is easily created falsely) as well as a toolkit for composing in various modes of communication, as well as a mode of thinking about reality. As they say, everything is an argument. As Plato has Socrates pose it in this dialogue, rhetoric is "a universal art of enchanting the mind by arguments."

Practiced rhetoricians of the ancient world, such as the Sophists, taught the art of rhetoric without a mind for ethics. By and large, the Sophists were well-paid tutors who could teach a person to make a lesser cause seem the greater. We come now to the passage that opens this chapter. It brings us full circle, to the relationship between rhetoric and philosophy as Plato presents it to us:

**Socrates:** Let us put the matter thus: Suppose that I persuaded you to buy a horse and go to the wars. Neither of us knew what a horse was like, but I knew that you believed a horse to be of tame animals the one which has the longest ears.

**Phaedrus:** That would be ridiculous.

**Socrates:** There is something more ridiculous coming: Suppose, further, that in sober earnest I, having persuaded you of this, went and composed a speech in honor of an ass, whom I entitled a horse beginning: "A noble animal and a most useful possession, especially in war, and you may get on his back and fight, and he will carry baggage or anything."

**Phaedrus:** How ridiculous!

**Socrates:** Ridiculous! Yes; but is not even a ridiculous friend better than a cunning enemy?

**Phaedrus:** Certainly.

**Socrates:** And when the orator instead of putting an ass in the place of a horse puts good for evil being himself as ignorant of their true nature as the city on which he imposes is ignorant; and having studied the notions of the multitude, falsely persuades them not about "the shadow of an ass," which he confounds with a horse, but about good which he confounds with evil—what will be the harvest which rhetoric will be likely to gather after the sowing of that seed?

**Phaedrus:** The reverse of good. [47]

More than two thousand years ago, the very same problems of disinformation, lies, and deception were plaguing the minds we have since placed at the center of Western thought and culture. It may not be such a bad idea, then, to return to these great thinkers to see what wisdom they may have drummed up in response to these problems. For Plato, at least, it was essentially in the relationship between rhetoric and philosophy that these problems could be solved. A person with a philosophical nature, who bothers to seek the truth about any subject on which they communicate, will not use rhetoric to spellbind minds in a false manner. A person who does not bother to drive toward the truth of a subject may use rhetoric to captivate audiences for the wrong reasons. At the very heart of Plato's thinking was this sense of ethics: that we owe ourselves the pursuit of truth, and that pursuit of truth is philosophy. Academic rhetoricians have been, of course, banging their heads against the wall the last decade or so with the resurgence of hot topic issues surrounding social media, fake news, and disinformation, saying, "Hey, we have a whole field of study that helps us deal with this already! It's called rhetoric!" but the themes of Platonic dialogues are not particularly sexy topics for cable news and mainstream media.

And frankly, the way I see it, rhetoricians have failed, at least in part, at their own art. It is not some fault of the public (whatever that may mean) that rhetoric (and philosophy, too, for that matter) has slipped away from us as a discipline. We have not been persuasive in making our field of study attractive enough to be considered seriously by most people. The jargon of rhetoric textbooks can be impenetrably dry and dense. They are filled with largely inconsequential scholarly disagreements between thinkers like Bitzer and Vatz. There are complex systemic and social issues for the erosion of rhetoric and philosophy, too, of course—from the design of public education curriculum to the anti-intellectualism movement in the United States and elsewhere.

I am again reminded of a fine insight from Tolkien, though this time it was more poignantly phrased in Peter Jackson's film adaptations of the famous fantasy novels. In the film *The Two Towers*, Faramir remarks, "The Shire must truly be a great realm, Master Gamgee, where gardeners are held in high honor." We can learn much about a people by observing who they idolize. What does it say about a nation when it has so few philosophers who are held in "high honor?" In Plato's *Republic,* Plato famously wonders what a world would look like with philosophers as kings. The text is ethically problematic for modern readers, but still, we are left wondering—what would a world look like that esteemed the truth over all else? Can we envision a world with philosophy as a serious priority?

Rhetoricians in antiquity walked among the highest orders of society. Can we dream of a world where philosophy and rhetoric are incorporated, once again, into public education? Would it completely solve the disinformation crisis? Perhaps not—but we have few other reasonable proposals, and with the rapid advancement of technologically facilitated disinformation and sophisticated hyper-targeted advertisements, we need to do something quickly to protect the liberty of our minds against the daily information warfare we are encountering.

In today's world, rhetoricians—that is, people who study rhetoric academically and historically—usually teach writing and are often not well paid for their work. I hope this book will revive rhetoric and its ancient aims for a broader audience. For our ancient philosophers, rhetoric was not just the use of empty language to prove a point. In fact, this was Plato's exact critique of the Sophists, who, he thought, were not taking language seriously enough. For Plato, the basis of rhetoric was an in alignment with the truth and the search for truth, for he understood the extraordinary power—and danger—of speech. The ancient Greek Sophist Gorgias, a speech-making rockstar of his day, compared the power of speech to that of a *pharmakon*, or drug, just as we have seen Plato do in *Phaedrus*. Wine, too, was often referred to with this same term of *pharmakon*, as wine was used as a delivery mechanism for more than ninety recorded and archived medicinal recipes. Plenty of contemporary scholars suspect this wine may have frequently been imbued with psychedelic substances. Ancient Greeks understood the power of language and its ability to change our reality through persuasion. They understood the ease with which a speaker could use these powers of language and persuasion for evil.

Ancient Greeks did not mince words about good or evil, either. Some things were good, and some were evil. In our age of moral relativity, we could learn something from closely investigating universals we might agree on: what happened at Auschwitz must be considered evil. How can we disagree on what must be axiomatic? If we cannot agree here, we render our language, and maybe our lives, meaningless. That's what is at stake with language and rhetoric. And that's just the start. Public education in the 2020s in the United States omits some of the most important fields of human study from its curriculum—namely, rhetoric and philosophy. For thousands of years, our ancestors studied and trained in the art of rhetoric, from the heyday of the Hellenistic golden age in the 300s BCE to well past the crumbling of the walls at Constantinople and the fall of the Eastern Roman Empire in the 1400s CE. Why, now, have we so callously decided that the study of life and language should be abandoned by the public?

In the United States, we are seeing a harvest of bad rhetoric. Language is decoupled from truth. We see intense political polarization across the country, state-sanctioned police violence against Black people, and an exploding degree of inequality, unemployment, and pain and suffering for millions of individuals and families. A *Time* magazine cover only half-jokingly named 2020 "The Worst Year Ever." The negative, painful daily experiences that so many humans suffer through, including hunger; joblessness; brokenness; lives spent sleeping in cars or on streets, stealing diapers for children; are the harvest of bad rhetoric. We are now reaping the seeds of evil and lies. But this is nothing new. Humanity has been reaping the seeds of evil and lies for thousands of years. Yet, it could be within our power to fortify ourselves against these ills by using the wisdom from the ancients that we see in Platonic dialogues like *Phaedrus*.

More recently, on January 6, 2021, after thousands of protesters overtook the Capitol Building in Washington, DC, Democratic Majority Leader Mike Schumer addressed the reconvened Senate. One woman was fatally shot, and at least twelve arrests were made that evening with hundreds more taking place over the subsequent months. After relative peace was restored to the capitol, Schumer blamed Donald Trump for inciting the riot and remarked that we were witnessing the results of a "demagogic" president. United States President Joe Biden reminded us of these dangers in his inaugural address in Washington DC on January 20, 2021: "Recent weeks and months have taught us a painful lesson. There is truth and there are lies. Lies told for power and for profit." These are fundamentally the same problems that Plato was dealing with in *Phaedrus*. We sometimes see the dangers of rhetoric-uncoupled-from-philosophy unfold right before our very eyes. This is why persuasive speech must always be kept in check through an alignment toward truth.

When my students doubt the significance of rhetoric or the power of speech, I remind them of some of the most significant tragedies humans have ever inflicted upon themselves. For example, Adolf Hitler's extraordinary power of persuasion—as well as his effective use of new systems of mass communication and air transport, which were arguably a part of a rhetorical strategy—allowed him to spellbind a nation and lead it into war and genocide. This is precisely what Plato tried to warn us about thousands of years ago. That's the danger of speech without ethics. Hitler was an expert orator, but a miserable philosopher. There is something in a human that makes us susceptible to powerful speech, to the rise and fall of a voice, to passionate yelling and articulate turns of phrase. We are, perhaps, more emotional, more subject to magic, and stranger than we yet realize.

We've been talking about something very nebulous and abstract, this notion of truth, these faraway places, but I want to leave you with something useful. Aristotle set out a concrete definition of truth in *Metaphysics*. You can meditate on this for a while: "to say of what is that it is, and of what is not that it is not, is true." There's some food for thought, anyway. You could spend a whole afternoon working that over in your head, or at least the duration of a good shower and a long walk.

We can also end with one more important passage from *Phaedrus* before we pass on to our next set of stories and ideas from the ancient world. About halfway through the dialogue in which Plato talks of the relationship between rhetoric, philosophy, and deception, there is a very interesting exchange between Socrates and Phaedrus. In this sequence, Plato is asking how we can fortify ourselves against deception. The answer is through philosophy, Socrates asserts. We must know the truth of a subject so as not to be deceived. Again, what is truth? It's such a slippery question, but a good one. Well, we will continue to consider perspectives on that question as we go along. But for now, consider these words:

> **Socrates:** Let me put the matter thus: When will there be more chance of deception-when the difference is large or small?
> **Phaedrus:** When the difference is small.
> **Socrates:** And you will be less likely to be discovered in passing by degrees into the other extreme than when you go all at once?
> **Phaedrus:** Of course.

**Socrates:** He, then, who would deceive others, and not be deceived, must exactly know the real likenesses and differences of things?

**Phaedrus:** He must.

**Socrates:** And if he is ignorant of the true nature of any subject, how can he detect the greater or less degree of likeness in other things to that of which by the hypothesis he is ignorant?

**Phaedrus:** He cannot.

**Socrates:** And when men are deceived and their notions are at variance with realities, it is clear that the error slips in through resemblances?

**Phaedrus:** Yes, that is the way.

**Socrates:** Then he who would be a master of the art must understand the real nature of everything; or he will never know either how to make the gradual departure from truth into the opposite of truth which is effected by the help of resemblances, or how to avoid it?

**Phaedrus:** He will not.

**Socrates:** He then, who being ignorant of the truth aims at appearances, will only attain an art of rhetoric which is ridiculous and is not an art at all?

**Phaedrus:** That may be expected. [48]

To uncover more of our difficult relationship with truth, we will go back in time next, even further, more than four thousand years ago, to the first named author that we have in human history. Her name was Enheduanna, The High Priestess, a poet, princess, priestess, and someone who provides a series of clues about the early human relationship with truth, reality, and the universe that we carry with us to this day.

*Figure 5: 19th Century Statue of a Greek Slave, by Hiram Powers - Smithsonian American Art Museum, 1968.155.109 - Modeled 1841-1843*

*Figure 6: Bust of Socrates*

HOMER 800-701 BCE

DRACO - FIRST WRITTEN LAWS IN ATHENS, EARLY
DEMOCRACY 621 BCE

GREEKS MINT FIRST COINS 600 BCE

GORGIAS 483-375 BCE

SOCRATES 470-399 BCE

PELOPONNESIAN WARS 431-405 BCE

PLATO 427-327 BCE

PLATO'S ACADEMY FOUNDED 386 BCE

ARISTOTLE 384-322 BCE

ALEXANDER THE GREAT 356-323 BCE

ROMANS DEFEAT GREEKS AT CORINTH 146 BCE

BATTLE OF ACTIUM, END OF HELLENISTIC ERA 31 BCE

I HAVE TOLD YOUR FURY TRULY.

—Enheduanna [49]

## CHAPTER V

# "Let the Flood Come Down the Mountain": Enheduanna and the Origins of Writing

*Like a dragon,*
*You poisoned the land—*
*When you roared at the earth*
*In your thunder,*
*Nothing green could live.*
*A flood fell from the mountain...*
—ENHEDUANNA [50]

## THE BIRTH OF THE WORD

It's hard to imagine a time when writing simply didn't exist. It certainly would make remembering things a bit difficult; imagine going grocery shopping with no list or keeping track of all your appointments and relatives' birthdays with no calendar. Whether you use a smartphone to organize your life, or you write your grocery list down on a sheet of paper, it's all mediated with the technology of writing. We have become the species that writes. But we weren't always like this. For Plato, as we see at the end of the dialogue *Phaedrus* (if you dare to venture to the end), writing would have been a relatively new technology for the ancient Greeks. For most of the time that humans have walked the Earth, we've been oral creatures, not textual creatures.

Plato was grumpy about writing in the same way that today's older generations sometimes question modern technological developments. Some version of "These kids and their smartphones!" has been uttered throughout every epoch of history. "I can't stand these horseless carriages clogging up the streets!" And we can't dismiss these critiques altogether. Not all our technologies benefit us. Better to critique them. Plato had some interesting arguments against writing, certainly—and it was a truly revolutionary technology that would have seemed quite disruptive to a primarily oral culture. Remember that the ancient Greeks were lovers of epic poetry and giving speeches, and they revered the power of the stage. This critique of writing comes at the very end of *Phaedrus*, in the section I sometimes refer to as "The Myth of Theuth." Here, Socrates invents a myth about the origins of writing. Socrates goes on to warn us that writing could harm our memory, and that writing was just a shadowy representation of the true thoughts in our minds. This, in many ways, mirrors Plato's understanding of the Ideal Forms. In the same way that any circle you draw is just a shadow of the Ideal Form of a perfect circle, any idea that we write down on the page is just a distant shadow of the pure form of the thought in our minds. And Plato has Socrates go on to compare writing to painting; it could not respond, it was static. For, in Plato's view, the highest standard of language use was the dialogue, the conversation, the living language. Philosophy, for Plato, was an embodied and living experiment that was acted out between people.

Writing completely reshaped humanity and our potential to communicate across time and space. All our modern technologies rely on this symbolic form of communication. Writing developed in parallel with our early civilizations. Likely, the particular challenges of complex society led to the simultaneous development of writing systems in Sumer and Egypt about five thousand years ago, around 3400-3100 BCE, and seemingly independently in Mesoamerica and China about two thousand years after that. In other words, humans started to conduct transactions, make deals, wage war, and think about stars and gods and where they came from, and they needed a way to communicate those ideas to other humans. For example, "I am giving you ten goats and I would like a record of that transaction" could suddenly be documented with early Sumerian cuneiform. That's a technological revolution if there ever was one. Cuneiform was an early type of writing that involved using a wedge to write symbols in clay tablets, and it transformed human history forever.

Language and writing are very different beasts. Spoken language may have developed as far back as one hundred thousand years ago (though scholars disagree on many of the important details, such as how the Cognitive Revolution which enabled language actually began), while writing developed a long time after that, nearly simultaneously in ancient Sumer and Egypt. We have a different kind of symbol use, what we informally refer to as cave paintings, that crop up around forty-to-sixty thousand years ago. Our oldest musical instruments, bone flutes, also date to this time: around sixty thousand years. This seems to be the era of the

Cognitive Revolution, when humans first began involving themselves with symbols, stories, art, and ritual. It might be more accurately called a Cultural Revolution.

But written language took much, much longer to come around. It's birth comes tens of thousands of years after the cave paintings. One of the most remarkable illustrations of the essential difference between language and writing can be seen in developmental psychology. We can see it plainly even in the casual observation of how children learn. My daughter, now three-years-old, did not require any special instruction in learning how to speak. Her first word was "bird." She would point out our front window in the living room at a chicadee or other friendly neighborhood bird and happily shout "bird, bird!" We took her to the Lake Superior Zoo in nearby Duluth, MN so she could see many more types of birds. It wasn't long after that—as if by magic, before my very eyes—that she began to speak polysyllabic words. Then, she began to form short phrases. Pretty soon, she was singing songs and telling us what she wanted for breakfast! My son, now two, is catching up. Right now he's fixated on the words "cake" and "donut," after we indulged in some sweets for his second birthday party.

The illustration of the difference, though, comes in the difficulty that comes with identifying letters and in understanding that they represent sounds—indeed that when they're put together, they represent the very words that our children already know how to say and understand. Giving a three-year-old a writing utensil is basically asking for disaster. If not in our own home, we've all seen streaks of crayon colored on a wall somewhere. While spoken language comes naturally (even joyfully) to a child, the practice of writing comes only with patience, instruction, and no small amount of repetition and discomfort. We naturally learn how to speak. We are oral creatures. We do not easily learn to read and write. We must be taught how to use the symbolic representation systems of language.

Now imagine this divide between spoken language and writing happening at a larger scale across civilization. It's no wonder that as late as 370 BCE, Plato's *Phaedrus* recorded Socrates's concerns that writing was a problematic technology—one that could hinder our memories, and lacked the dynamic, interactive power of dialogue. Of course, it's ironic that these ideas only come to us because of the invention of writing. Still, Socrates's critique of writing comes to us almost three thousand years after the Sumerians began the practice. This shows just how slow humans can be to adopt new technologies and encourage their spread from one area of the globe to another. Julian Fellowes's excellent television series *Downton Abbey* explores some of these themes through depictions of English life in the early twentieth century, a period when the working class and wealthy landowners had to deal with rapidly changing times and new technologies. The automobile, telephone, gramophone, wireless radio, and the powerful weapons of the first World War came rushing at them, changing their lives dramatically. Some characters adapt to these changes with excitement, some with innovation, some with reservation, and some with resistance. We all know someone in our life who is still a bit clunky with a computer and refuses to get a smart phone. They're neither right nor wrong to resist; to each their own.

The German philosopher Martin Heidegger wrote brilliantly about technology in his essay, "The Question Concerning Technology." Heidegger warns us that we have been fooled by technology, thinking of it only in terms of what it can do for us and what we can do with it. If you ask someone: "What's the purpose of a hammer?" they will almost certainly answer, "To hammer nails!" But for Heidegger, this is not the whole picture. The real purpose of the hammer is to open a possibility of living in a world where things can be hammered, and with this possibility, the human relationship with the world fundamentally shifts. With a hammer, you can build houses, churches, and schools, for example. Now, you live in a world that has physical manifestations of institutions and systems of power, a world that is fundamentally different than the one which predated the hammer. Or, perhaps now you live in a world where a person is expected to build a house, because hammers are widely available—so now you must change your way of life and get a job at a factory so you can buy a plot of land to build your house and get married, because without a house, you won't attract a partner. It's all connected. The hammer is not just a means to an end—it has a host of unintended consequences that result from its existence. The hammer does much more than just allow for the pounding of nails. The hammer fundamentally changes our relationship with the world by reshaping our world as one in which things can be hammered. And might the factory that produces hammers then go on and create waste which contributes to global climate change? Perhaps. Even a simple technology like a hammer can have vast, unexpected, rippling effects in the world. And this can be said of any technology: writing, computers, automobiles, satellites, artificial intelligence, and whatever comes next. Certainly, our ancient friends had no idea that *writing* would one day be used to aid in the design and construction of rocket ships to take us to the moon, or to spread misinformation on social media.

A final illustration can be made about the vast difference between a written and an oral culture. Imagine the children's game that is often called "Telephone" (or the "Gossip Game" or "Rumor"). In a school setting, the teacher will have all the children in the class line up in a long row, several feet apart from each other. The teacher will whisper, very quietly, a complex sentence into the ear of the first child in the line: "Thirty-seven incredible elephants were spotted Northeast from the Dnieper River. The riders were nine feet tall, cloaked in houndstooth, and laden with daisies." The children whisper the secret phrase to each other, going down the line. Finally, when the last child in the line has heard the phrase, they repeat it aloud to the group. Everyone laughs as the teacher tells the group what the original phrase should have been. Without fail, some miscommunication happens during the course of the game, and the children learn a valuable lesson about credibility. Usually, the end result is nothing like the original; you would be lucky if even the mention of elephants survived to the end of the chain.

Imagine, then, the "Telephone" game across hundreds—or even thousands—of years, or across vast distances and varied landscapes as human nomads spread across the world. It wouldn't be a very reliable system for recording and sharing knowledge among groups of people. The technology of writing has, for better or worse, enabled our very particular types of cultures and societies and made possible all the scientific, industrial, technical, and technological advancements and violences that we've mustered up so far, from cars and computers, to missiles and MacBooks. As Carl Sagan once elegantly put it: "If you wish to make an apple pie from scratch, you must first invent the universe." So, too, if you wish to leave Earth's atmosphere in a rocket, you first need a society that can store and transmit information—in our case, via writing. Once you have writing, then you can come up with computers and the rest of the bits.

Or perhaps this is just a bias. We can amuse ourselves by imagining an oral society that transmits technical data and equations via epic poetry, like an MIT-educated Homer. The 2016 science fiction film *Arrival*, directed by Denis Villeneuve, is a great exercise in imagining how writing and language could manifest from non-human species.[51] In the film, an alien form of written language is depicted in a three-dimensional, multi-tendril, almost sculptural form. In an interview with NPR, Jessica Coon, a linguist who was consulted for the screenplay of *Arrival*, describes what the film may have gotten right or wrong about linguistics and its speculations on alien language. Coon explains how the Sapir-Whorf hypothesis, which posits that the language we speak shapes our perception of the world, has passed out of favor among linguists. There now seems to be an agreement among scholars that the extent to which language determines our perception of the world is limited. A person who speaks Spanish and a person who speaks English do not experience life differently because of the language they speak. I'm, of course, left to wonder, though—what if we were thinking about a vastly different language, fundamentally different in its grammar, like the language of the species from another planet, an entirely different language tree? Well, always fun to dream about aliens and other worlds. And what does propaganda and disinformation look like on other planets?

To get back on the case, historically and anthropologically, this is all quite significant. Humans are not very good at imagining the past. We tend to think of people who lived thousands of years ago as hunter-gatherers or cavepeople, bashing each other with rocks—probably no thanks to Hollywood and cartoon depictions of early humans as unintelligent and scruffy. But the humans who lived one thousand years ago, and for that matter, the humans who lived 24,781 years ago, were likely not much different from us. They would have felt hunger and pain. They would have told stories and made music. They would feel tired, get excited, dance, and cook. The fundamentals of what constitute human life were very much present thousands of years ago, as they are today. And, as we have noted through the works of rhetoricians like George Kennedy, we have been lying to each other and persuading each other the entire time.

This is even more evident in the early civilizations of Mesopotamia, where the first named author wrote poems and songs of love, harvest, praise, and power. What scholars have largely gotten wrong about the world's first named author, however, is her status as a first-rate propagandist, in service of her father's growing empire. I am speaking, of course, about the ancient priestess-poet, Enheduanna. In Enheduanna's poetry—the oldest-written lyric lines that have survived through time—we see so much humanity that it almost transports us across time to the walled city-state of Ur in ancient Sumer. We can imagine a bustling city of men and women wearing brightly dyed skirts or kilts called kaunake, dancing at a festival, or sowing seeds in the shadow of a defensive structure that towered up from the walls of the city. Let us go back in time even further than we have traveled yet—more than two thousand years before Plato lived—to the ancient land of Mesopotamia. To put this in perspective: the amount of time is roughly the same between Enheduanna's life and Plato's life as it is between today's date and the time of Plato.

## PROPAGANDA AT THE BIRTH OF CIVILIZATION

The first named author in all human history—at least, the first we currently know of whose work has survived—was the daughter of an ancient king. She was a poet and a priestess. Enheduanna is a name that should stir in our hearts a sense of mystery, of far-gone lands and a way of life that may seem, at first, unfamiliar to our own. She lived approximately 4,300 years ago in the walled city-state of Ur (in present-day Iraq). Her father, Sargon of Akkad, was the stuff of legend: a conqueror, military strategist, and grand ruler on an epic scale. He may have been the first ancient human to rule over, what we would consider in contemporary terms, an Empire. And in the foundation of these first empires, we see some of the first major artifacts of disinformation and propaganda.

An important shift in ancient thinking occurred when poetry and language were harnessed to deify kings and rulers. It's likely no coincidence that we see the first explicit uses of propaganda in the world's first empires. People are not gods, of course. Even the greatest kings that ever walked the Earth were just humans like the rest of us, with fallible minds and temporary bodies. However, the ways they deliberately controlled their public image (through their manner of dress, the choreography of soldiers on parade, the use of art and visual imagery in statues and stonework, and in the crafting of speeches, poetry, and language), are not dissimilar to methods employed by our contemporary politicians when they are trying to sway the public. After all, we still mint coins with the faces of our rulers on them, and we are easily persuaded by sharp suits and stage presence.

The results of the first televised presidential debate in America are a phenomenal testament to the sheer persuasive power of appearance. The common retelling goes that American citizens who listened to the John F. Kennedy and Richard Nixon debate of 1960 on their radio thought that Nixon had clearly won the debate and presented his ideas more effectively. But those who watched the debate on television found candidate Kennedy more convincing. Kennedy would go on to win the election and become the thirty-fifth president of the United States, serving in that role until his assassination in 1963. The ancient Roman rhetorician Quintilian explained how "the mere look of a man can be persuasive," and we now have countless peer-reviewed, academic studies that provide evidence for this. But we will talk more about mass media and then contemporary digital communications in relation to disinformation later in this book. For now, it's worth noting that many of these same, ancient techniques are still being used to lead people astray today. Imagine, for example, the people of North Korea who are propagandized to celebrate their Supreme Leader as a deity or godlike figure. The paradigm mirrors ancient Samaria, where Sumerians would have been tricked into thinking King Sargon had divine powers or was appointed by god—Enheduanna had been appointed by King Sargon to write the many temple hymns that survive to us as extant tablets. In many crucial ways, our practices are not entirely different in the United States, where celebrities, politicians, and entrepreneurs enjoy a kind of mythical status and use all the tricks and trappings of ancient persuasion and modern public relations to spread their messages, likenesses, and identities into our lives.

In her introduction to *Inanna: A New English Version,* Kim Echlin documents a significant shift in ancient literature between the Old Sumerian Phase and the Neo-Sumerian Phase. She writes that from 2500 to 2200 BCE, our ancient literature—particularly hymns, verse, and poetry—was mostly focused on the spiritual celebration of deities and their temples. There is much richness and nuance in this, as we will see in the work of Enheduanna, who employs anaphora, repetition, antithesis, and metaphor. In some ways, these surviving poems from the ancient priestess

Enheduanna look very modern. But to what purpose were these rhetorical devices first employed? In the Neo-Sumerian Phase that followed from 2200 to 1900 BCE, we first see "Sacred and royal literature begin to merge with deification of kings." [52] That is, the world's first emperors learned the value of controlling messaging around their image—something we might think of today as "building one's personal brand" or "brand identity" if we want to incorporate terminology from the world of marketing and advertising. Even before we began to see the deification of kings in literature, Enheduanna's father, King Sargon had "placed the name of a star" before his name to "symbolize [his] divine character." [53] And this was only one of many strategies that Sargon I used to build his image alongside the successful building of his empire. In short, it's hard not to see parallels between the building of the world's first empire and the world's first well-documented use of propaganda. To subjugate and rule over hundreds of thousands or millions of people, a ruler must carefully craft a particular image through every and any means necessary.

Philip Taylor, in his historical survey of propaganda, *Munitions of the Mind: A History of Propaganda from the Ancient World to the Present Day*, describes how the earliest forms of propaganda may date back even further than the first empires:

> "Anthropological and archaeological research suggests that before speech (organized language) all communication was visual. Primitive man communicated non-verbally via gestures and signals although sounds – cries and drumbeats, for instance – were also important. Tribal man developed masks, war cries, and threatening gestures both to frighten his enemies and impress his friends." [54]

Masks continue to be a topic of contentious debate in the United States since the COVID-19 pandemic disrupted all our lives. But in many cultures, mask-wearing when sick is simply seen as considerate and normative. And of course, there are both ancient and modern cultures where inventive and artistic masks are used for manifold purposes: to transform the self into something else, for ritual and festival, or to embody the form of a deity. Masks, in this way, can be tools of disinformation and persuasion. Indeed, as Taylor suggests, ancient masks may have been used in early warfare to "frighten" one's "enemies." The mask transforms reality and changes one's state of being. It changes the way others perceive us. Masks have been an integral part of human culture, experience, storytelling, and mythology, whether in ancient Greek and Roman tragedy or comedy, Japanese Noh Drama, or the life and war of early, pre-writing societies. [55]

Taylor tells us more about early forms of visual intimidation and propaganda:

"Margaret Mead, the famous anthropologist of the inter-war years whose studies *Coming of Age in Samoa* and *Growing Up in New Guinea* throw much light on the behavior of primitive peoples, suggests that visual symbols were used for very specific purposes. For example, one village might send a message to another in the form of leaves and weapons arranged in such a way as to suggest a danger from a third village, thereby hoping to forge an alliance. Equally, 'the omission of some small formal act of courtesy was, in earlier times in Samoa, the possible signal for an outbreak of hostilities between two villages... It is only in Neolithic cave drawings from about 7000 BC that we see men using weapons against each other, making these drawings perhaps the earliest form of war propaganda. As the old saying has it, a picture speaks a thousand words."[56]

With Taylor's help, we can start to imagine that time some seven-to-ten thousand years ago when the nomadic, hunter-gatherer humans first began to form agricultural communities through the art of husbandry in the cultivation of crops and domesticated animals. Following this shift in community organization, it did not take humans long to invent weapons of warfare—the sling and the bow and arrow, for example—which necessitated the building of walls and serious military and defensive architectural strategy. As early as 5,000 BCE we have evidence of massive defensive walls with strategically placed towers, likely used to keep out the aggression of other peoples. Taylor writes that "the wall at Uruk was eventually nearly 6 miles long with over 900 towers, supposedly the work of the legendary king, Gilgamesh." Walls would continue to be a defining feature of human settlements for thousands of years, effectively until the fall of Constantinople in 1453, which also marked the end of the Eastern Roman Empire. It was at this sacking of Constantinople that enormous cannons were used to destroy the once-impenetrable walls, effectively rendering useless any future wall-building. The technology of war has a way of dramatically influencing human activities. Our present predicament with nuclear weapons and the deadlock of mutually assured destruction (MAD) is a prime example for our thought experiments. Undoubtedly, some future technologies will make possible other weapons which render many of our present practices unnecessary or obsolete.

# ENHEDUANNA AND THE DISINFORMATION OF AN EMPIRE

Enheduanna's poetry in praise of divine, imaginary beings still echoes to this day. She used rhetorical strategies and pathos to such effect that it's not hard to imagine how her style influenced other high priests, priestesses, military thinkers, and rulers. While most scholars write in praise of Enheduanna, we should not forget that she was fundamentally a propagandist. She was commissioned by her father to write forty-two Temple Hymns to celebrate the various religious sites of the empire and to encourage citizens to participate in religious life. Enheduanna was working in the service of the empire, weaving propaganda and willfully disinforming the public about powerful gods and goddesses who did not exist. This is just one of the many problems we face when trying to enrich the canon of rhetoric; we are quick to praise new voices, but we sometimes forget the social, cultural, and historical context around the figures. In rhetoric, this is a question of *purpose*. What were the purposes of Enheduanna's poetry? To inspire religious sentiment and encourage worship of the empire's gods and goddesses. To subdue the public to religious service. And ultimately, to fortify King Sargon's power as ruler of the empire.

In Jane Hirshfield's translation of "The Hymn to Inanna," we see Enheduanna wielding immense lyrical power in a direct address to the goddess Inanna:

"O winged Lady,
Like a bird
You scavenge the land.
Like a charging storm

You charge,
Like a roaring storm
You roar,
You thunder in thunder,
Snort in rampaging winds." [57]

To today's reader, who has likely been exposed to all manner of violent and graphic video content from film, television, and other media, we may wonder what the big deal is about this poetry. But we must remember that Enheduanna is the first named poet in all human history, and that writing—the very art of scratching symbols into tablets—was a very new invention. Enheduanna is conjuring an image of a deity that is both destructive and benevolent. Remember, in ambiguity, propaganda is most effective—when we hear a slogan like "Support our troops!' it is hard for us to find a reason to fight against the cause, even if it is used to bolster an argument for an unjust or unethical military conflict. This is how propaganda functions. So, too, with Enheduanna—why not submit to a goddess who is both loving and powerful, who is both like a bird and like a dragon, who is both the storm that can destroy us and the rain that gives life to our crops? In crafting such rhetorically powerful imagery, Enheduanna was able to leave us a rich legacy of poetic technique and devices and, through her propaganda production, was able to solidify her own long career as high priestess and aid in the consolidation of King Sargon's power.

Thousands of years later, the rhetorical techniques of lyric and poetry seen in Enheduanna's work are still being used. We hear music and lyrics at political rallies and in political video advertisements on social media and in mass-media broadcasts. In the speeches of politicians and the members of the ruling classes, we hear many of the same rhetorical techniques and ideas that were used by our ancient Sumerian friends: repetition, parallelism, anaphora, and antithesis to name just a few. But we also see this significant strategy of deifying the human and transforming the human into something that he or she is not. Through elevated stages, arbitrary costume (like suits and ties), staged photography and videography, and a myriad of other tricks, the contemporary politician does not look too different from the ancient warlord king who attempted to shape his public perception and persuade the public about his status and abilities. All these tricks constitute disinformation. No human is a god, after all. But these forms of disinformation and propaganda were used to control the masses, to spread fear and intimidate others, and to maintain power in ancient societies, much the same way they are used today. What more could a ruler want than an adoring population who worships them like a superhuman entity?

For Philip Taylor, propaganda is made up of "the conscious, methodical and planned decisions to employ techniques of persuasion designed to achieve specific goals that are *intended to benefit those organizing the process* [emphasis added]."[58]

Don Fallis offers specific examples of contemporary disinformation, such as "deceptive advertising (in business and in politics), government propaganda, doctored photographs, forged documents, fake maps, internet frauds, fake websites, and manipulated Wikipedia entries."[59] Put more succinctly, Fallis argues that disinformation is "misleading information that has the function of misleading."

It is in this light that we see many examples from the ancient world—ancient rulers certainly benefited by disinformation that would lift their image to divine status. It is difficult for us to tease out, however, whether someone like Enheduanna was more of an artist or more of a propagandist. We cannot know the extent to which her religious fervor was genuine, nor to what extent it was consciously employed as a tool to corral a rowdy population into thinking and believing in alignment with the state to consolidate power under her father, King Sargon. We will never know the true intentions of ancient peoples, but we can study the effects of their decisions and consider what benefits they may have received from their actions in an attempt to reverse engineer their propaganda and communication campaigns.

Some of the most salient examples of disinformation in human history are related to this process of the deification of a ruler as a justification for positions of power. George Kennedy, in writing about the propaganda program of Akhenaton (Ikhnaton), the Egyptian ruler wedded to Nefertiti, describes how he traces an "official rhetoric" to the time period by examining how those "in power sought to solidify their position, not only by means of spoken and written words, but by calling on the aid of art, architecture, and religious institutions." [60] Akhenaton's reign, however, was a political trainwreck, and his propaganda program ultimately resulted in failure. Akhenaton was hostile to the priests of Amon in Thebes, and intended on replacing them with priests in service to the sun god Aton. Kennedy writes that the ruler even changed his name from Amonhotep ("Amon is Satisfied") to Akhenaton ("He Who Serves Aton") among other significant propaganda tactics, such as "the founding of a new capital, far from Thebes, the encouraging of naturalistic art, and the composition of poetry celebrating Aton." [61]

Throughout human history, these very same tactics have proved incredibly useful, such as when the ancient Roman emperor Constantine promoted Christianity by ordering Roman

soldiers to paint religious symbols on their shields and by relo-
cating the capital to Constantinople. Akhenaton's propaganda
failure probably tells us more about the entrenched power of the
ancient priests than it does about the citizens' ability to resist
disinformation and weaponized messaging—throughout the ancient world, the struggle between the church and the state was
more palpable than it is today (though we still struggle in all
places in the world with the interference of religion in government). Kennedy writes, "With Akhenaton's death the priests of
Amon reasserted their power, the capital returned to Thebes, and
Egyptian art returned to a traditional style." [62]

In summarizing his survey on rhetoric in the ancient Near
East, Kennedy writes that "As in nonliterate societies, rhetoric in
the ancient Near East was primarily a tool of transmitting and
defending traditional political, social, and religious values." [63]
Now, more than ever, we should remember to value our free
speech and our ability to speak against those in power, whether
that means we are speaking against corporations, big business,
our governments and political leaders, or, increasingly, those who
have their hands both in the pots of legislation as well as big
business. For much of human history, rhetoric was used to control, propagandize, and disinform. While this is still the case today, due to the incredible sacrifices and risks of those before us,
we continue to have the extraordinary freedom to think, speak,
write, and transmit what we think, feel, and desire without fear
of death or torture.

In a surprisingly optimistic passage from political activist and
linguist Noam Chomsky, he writes that the American "dissident
culture survived," and that there are indeed signs of a "civilizing
effect, despite all the propaganda, despite all the efforts to control thought and manufacture consent." [64] Perhaps the major

political moments of the American 1960s and 1970s, such as the feminist movement, the environmental movement, and anti-nuclear movement, have born gradual changes in our consciousness that have set the stage for us in the 2020s and beyond. I see the same effect that Chomsky writes of, now multiplied: "Skepticism about power has grown, and attitudes have changed on many, many issues. It's kind of slow, maybe even glacial, but perceptible and important."[65] To zoom out further gives us a better sense of the progress. Our world today is much different from ancient Egyptian and Sumerian cities where propaganda and indoctrination would just be matters of fact. In those societies, citizens had few tools and little education to encourage them to unravel disinformation programs. In these ancient cities (in some ways so like present-day North Korea in the deification of the leader and absolute manufacture of consent), when you are told to worship your leader as a god, you do it, whether you believe it in your heart or not. To not worship the leader as a god was punishable by death. So, you go ahead and do it. And the very basis of life is formed on a lie, a deception. It corrupts a society and obscures the very possibility of democracy, change, and progress.

Some of the earliest records of human writing were closer to what we consider today to be accounting, or perhaps we might categorize them as technical writing. The ancient Sumerians used their cuneiform system to create receipts and keep tally of exchanges: thirty bushels of wheat, seven head of oxen, and so on. With Enheduanna's poetry, we see the first record of poetic and rhetorical strategies in action. Some of the characteristics of Enheduanna's style are still very much in use today in our literary language, political speeches, and even in marketing and advertising. In Enheduanna, we see examples of repetition, parallelism, metaphor, symbolism, and allusion, just to name a few of the rhetorical devices or techniques that are on display. For example, we see Enheduanna write in the second stanza of the "Hymn to Inanna":

Like a dragon,
You poisoned the land—
When you roared at the earth
In your thunder,
Nothing green could live.
A flood fell from the mountain:
You, Inanna,
Foremost in Heaven and Earth.
Lady riding a beast,
You rained fire on the heads of men.
Taking your power from the Highest,
Following the commands of the Highest,
Lady of all the great rites,
Who can understand all this is yours? [66]

We see the antithesis (or juxtaposition of opposites in prose) of "Heaven and Earth." Antithesis can be seen in famous examples from literature, such as in those well-known opening lines from Charles Dickens in his *A Tale of Two Cities*, "It was the best of times, it was the worst of times." We see antithesis frequently in political speeches, such as in this antithetical construction in the opening to President Joe Biden's "State of the Union Address" delivered on March 1, 2022: "Last year, COVID-19 kept us apart. This year, we're finally together again." [67] Rhetorical devices are so commonly found in political speeches that it took me just two minutes to find this example of antithesis from perusing the transcripts of modern political speeches. The point here is that our ancient thinkers and writers used, identified, and set down a particular style of persuasive language that we still carry with us today. Where there are more tricky questions is whether there is something inherently persuasive about some of these devices or whether we have become enculturated and accustomed to be persuaded by them. I suspect there is a bit of both at play here. The significance of repetition likely has strong evolutionary and neurobiological underpinnings—it is all the easier for us to remember something that we have heard multiple times, and we are lovers of patterns. Repetition in speech is a sonic pattern. The same might be said about antithesis, which plays on our natural abilities to spot differences and to discern between values in nature—the categorical nature of human thinking and, again, our interest in pattern and logic lights up our brain when we see the opportunity to contrast two concepts.

We see simile when Inanna is described as being "Like a dragon," which offers in itself a book's worth of unpacking and analysis. Scholars are still working on what might be called the Dragon Problem, which is also a fun thought experiment: is it merely a coincidence that the dragon, a prominent figure in human mythological bestiary, is so like a creature that actually walked on our planet millions of years ago, the dinosaur? Is there something hard-wired into our evolutionary memory to be awed and afraid by giant reptiles, some remnant of memory from long-distant ancestors whose brain structures are still present? Or is it more likely that myths of dragons began in human society when humans came across massive skeletal remains—if even those of whales—and speculated what fantastic beasts might have lived here? It's certainly a puzzle, and there's no shortage of interesting material to investigate in this regard. But we see here in Enheduanna this allusion to the mythical creature of the

.dragon, and still today, the dragon is as prominent as ever, in films from Peter Jackson's adaption of J.R.R. Tolkien's *The Hobbit* to the hit series *Game of Thrones* based on George R.R. Martin's *A Song of Ice and Fire* series. Simile, metaphor, and analogy are extraordinarily effective teaching tools, and they're a way to render the indescribable into understandable terms. How better to frame the fury of a goddess than to describe her like a mighty dragon? And what better way to corral and control a population than to strike fear into their hearts? From four thousand years ago to today, this imagery still works us over and is effective. And we continue to see fear—remember the rhetorical appeal of *pathos*—as a useful tool in the contemporary politician's toolkit.

But more realistically, these figures, devices, and techniques of speech that we first see recorded by Enheduanna are likely the product of thousands of years—perhaps tens of thousands of years—of unrecorded oral culture which began sometime around forty-to-sixty thousand years ago during the Cognitive and Cultural Revolution. Around this time, we began to see the first human musical instruments and cave paintings. As documentary filmmaker Werner Herzog observes in *Cave of Forgotten Dreams*, an exploration of the archaeology and history of the Chauvet Caves of France, these early cave paintings were almost movie-like in their depiction of movement. They were likely drawn by firelight and intended to be observed in firelight. When holding a torch near the wall, we can recreate this effect of motion. Flames flicker and dance and shadows and light are cast, causing the drawings of bison, animals, and spear hunters to seem to move on the walls of the cave. This Cognitive and Cultural Revolution, which is largely inexplicable still, seems to have been the beginning of our art, culture, language, and music. From thousands of years of storytelling and oral communication, rhetoric was born.

The use of imagery, repetition, antithesis, anaphora, and similar devices are just as likely tools for the memorization of stories and epic poetry as they are tools intended for the persuasion of an audience—again, the reality usually lies somewhere in the middle—we don't want to commit a fallacy of a false dichotomy, a kind of "black or white" thinking. Storytellers used these rhetorical devices to memorize stories, but these same tools of memorization also proved to have strong effects on listeners, and in that synergistic relationship, a kind of oral and sonic storytelling feedback loop, our ancient oral tradition, was born. Early humans loved a good story. We still do.

You don't even need to know Old English to hear the rhetorical devices in the opening lines of a poem like the classic epic *Beowulf* from circa 900 CE:

Hwæt! We Gardena in geardagum,
þeodcyninga, þrym gefrunon,
hu ða æþelingas ellen fremedon.
Oft Scyld Scefing sceaþena þreatum,
monegum mægþum, meodosetla ofteah,
egsode eorlas... [68]

The pronunciation of the first line, in non-scholarly phonetic, sounds something like "What! Whey yar-dane-ugh, en yar-dah-goom." The second line is something like "They-ode-chin-ing-ugh, they-room geff-roon-on." Just to give you a sense of what it sounds like, if you're not big into Old English. Luckily, we live in the YouTube era, so you can go find a very real scholar of Old English read to it out for you and see what I mean. Just make sure it's someone who knows what they're doing; evaluate the source's credibility. The poem was probably set to music and sung, as many epic poems would have been. Benjamin Bagby has performed a particularly stylized and interesting interpretation that can be found online. The alliteration of "Gardena" and "gardagum" (both beginning with a kind of cartoon-pirate-like "Yarrr!" sound) is incredibly obvious, even if we do not speak or understand Old English, along with the alliteration in the second line of "þeodcyninga" and "þrym." Across languages, cultures, and time, rhetorical tools are used to tell stories, to spellbind audiences, and to create a particular kind of oratorical magic. These are precisely the type of rhetorical flourishes that ancient Greeks began to document and explain, such as in Gorgias's description of rhetoric that could act like a *pharmakon* upon us. We are spellbound by the magic of language and sounds.

There's a serious, salient lesson from Enheduanna's work, and it is that many of the techniques that were used thousands of years ago to persuade others are still in play today. In Enheduanna's work, for example, we see antithesis, which is just the fancy, rhetorical terminology for the juxtaposition of opposites. We know antithesis from classical literature ("It was the best of times, it was the worst of times..." from Charles Dickens). Other rhetorical techniques, called *anaphora* and *epistrophe,* are evident in Enheduanna's work. These are a type of repetition at the beginning of subsequent lines or clauses (anaphora) or at the end of subsequent lines (epistrophe). We also see in Enheduanna the use of metaphor and simile. These rhetorical devices have echoed through the ages and remain with us now, and we can readily find these rhetorical devices present in contemporary digital advertising and disinformation. As far back as the earliest named author, Enheduanna, and the world's first empire builder, King Sargon I, we see forms of disinformation and the art of persuasion taking center stage. It's no small coincidence that King

Sargon was able to build an empire when he had such powerful rhetorical techniques at his disposal—the use of imagery on the minted coins, the *stelae* which bore his name and inscriptions, the powerful religious poetry of his daughter Enheduanna—all of these were forms of disinformation to drug a population into a sleepy stupor, so that they would believe Sargon was a god-like figure who they should allow to rule over them. Stay in line, worship your rulers, and don't ask any questions. These are techniques that politicians and big corporate advertisers use all the time to persuade us. That's what the propagandists have been trying to tell us for thousands of years. But now, we can endeavor to understand their tools and techniques to decode and analyze their messages. We don't need to be spellbound any longer. We have rhetorical analysis to help us analyze messages across time, space, and media.

RHETORIC MAY BE DEFINED AS THE FACULTY OF OBSERVING IN ANY GIVEN CASE THE AVAILABLE MEANS OF PERSUASION.

—ARISTOTLE [69]

## CHAPTER VI

# Defending Against Disinformation: Aristotle and the System of Rhetoric

*Rhetoric may be defined as the faculty of observing in any given case the available means of persuasion. This is not a function of any other art. Every other art can instruct or persuade about its own particular subject-matter; for instance, medicine about what is healthy and unhealthy, geometry about the properties of magnitudes, arithmetic about numbers, and the same is true of the other arts and sciences. But rhetoric we look upon as the power of observing the means of persuasion on almost any subject presented to us; and that is why we say that, in its technical character, it is not concerned with any special or definite class of subjects.*

—ARISTOTLE [70]

So far, I have mostly been demonstrating the use of persuasion to mislead and control people: the dangers of persuasion. We've examined several instances of ancient disinformation and explicit propaganda, including examples from the present day. But all of this can be quite disheartening: "Yes, people in power lie to us, and have been lying to us for thousands of years. What shall we do about it, exactly? Isn't this just the way the world works? Those in power will maintain power at all costs, even if it means lying through their teeth." Of course, they will. That's why, if you want to live a rich, examined life where you try to ascertain the truth of things, you need to keep your eyes open and your rhetorical analysis glasses on as you make your way through the world.

Fortunately for us in these confused, "post-truth" times, the human pantheon has almost as long a legacy of truth-seekers as it does dis-informers. While those in power have attempted to persuade and lie to us, great thinkers have tried to work out systems for figuring out the truth and making sense of the universe. As far as we know, the ancient Greeks were the first human society to develop categorical systems of philosophy and the sciences and document their findings extensively. These early thinkers valued reason and observation and many ancient Greek philosophers were unafraid to challenge norms, customs, the people in power, and even the gods. Granted, challenging the gods may have been one step too far for Socrates, who was accused of corrupting the youth of Athens and impiety, or disrespecting the gods, though he denied this. Even in Plato's *Phaedrus* we see a reverence for the spiritual and the divine in the character of Socrates.

Those ancient days in the balmy, Mediterranean city-state of Athens were sometimes contentious and unstable. There were heroes and champions of freedom as well as tyrants and the greedy. Pericles may be one of the world's most unsung heroes; he went so far as to institute systems of democracy and usher in the Golden Age of ancient Greece by supporting the arts and promoting the right of all free men, not just the wealthy landowners, to vote. It didn't take long for a group of oligarchs known as the Thirty Tyrants to wrestle back control of the government and strip away the democratic freedoms instituted by Pericles. The struggle for democracy and freedom is as old as our societies. Nothing new under the sun. And it is in the suppression of democracy and the suppression of our freedoms that disinformation becomes so useful to the ruling classes.

While Socrates set a precedent for challenging the status quo, and his disciple Plato began to theorize, document, and archive philosophical dialogues which explored questions of justice and how to live a good life, it was Plato's disciple Aristotle who laid the building blocks for Western science and began building systems of thought—early scientific methodologies, we could rightly say—that still are important to humans today. Aristotle is widely credited with forming the basis for animal taxonomies and zoology, for example. He wrote on topics as diverse as ethics, poetics, politics, physics, biology, music, and more. But no man is an island. Aristotle joined Plato's school, The Academy, when he was just seventeen or eighteen, and stayed on for twenty years until he was in his late thirties. Aristotle would leave Plato's Academy when Plato died. As chance, fate, and the violence of history would have it, only about one third of Aristotle's manuscripts produced at his own school, The Lyceum, have survived through time. That a third of one person's work created the building blocks for all of science is impressive, to be sure. And the revival of Aristotle and Plato at the beginning of the Renaissance inspired millions across Europe. Then, thinkers like Thomas Aquinas revived Aristotle again in the beginnings of The Enlightenment. From there, technological revolutions and market economies sprouted the Industrial Revolution, and that takes us through the precarious twentieth century nearly to the present day. I'm getting ahead of myself, a bit, but it's no stretch to say that we owe much of human intellectual, cultural, scientific, and technological reality to the work of Aristotle.

Aristotle was a bit like the rebellious teenager in relation to Plato. While Plato was teaching about Ideal Forms and the colorless place at the edge of the universe, and waxing poetically about divine madness and ideal states, Aristotle was becoming interested in an approach based in material reality. "What about the world down here, on our planet?" Aristotle seemed to ask. He wanted to develop systems and methods for documenting observations. These are reductive comparisons, but we might say Plato was more interested in metaphysics while Aristotle was more interested in physics. Plato liked big ideas, while Aristotle liked details and classification. Plato imagined an ideal society from scratch in his *Republic*, while Aristotle largely concluded that people should be governed by careful ordering of laws.

But, of course, these are reductions. And where Aristotle figures into our present discussion is through his work on rhetoric, a topic that both he and Plato were interested in figuring out. Rhetoric, we now know dearly, is the ancient art of persuasion that was founded by the ancient Greeks. As classicist George Kennedy put it, the study of the persuasive use of language came out of a necessity. Ancient Athenians had to defend themselves in a court of law—something that interested Aristotle because of his insistence that laws were among the most important features of the social order. While Plato explored many of the philosophical and ethical dimensions of rhetoric in *Phaedrus*, Aristotle gave us more of a concrete framework to work with—Aristotle liked to break apart the subjects he was studying and create frameworks, heuristics, and taxonomies. While Plato made great progress in his explorations of the art of rhetoric, Aristotle took the reins from Plato to develop these ideas in a robust manner.

*Figure 7: This is "The School of Athens" by Raphael, painted between 1509-1511. It depicts Plato and Aristotle as the central figures. Plato is on the left with the bald head and long beard and his finger pointing to the sky, while Aristotle is on the right with the cropped beard and hand extended outward. This painting reduces the approaches of Plato and Aristotle to easy-to-understand visual imagery. Plato was mostly concerned with metaphysics—the big ideas, the world beyond, the Ideal Forms, the stuff at the very edges of the cosmos, which is why he is pointing up toward the sky, the great beyond. Aristotle was mostly concerned with the natural world, with physics as opposed to metaphysics—the material reality in front of us, the plants and animals and humans, the observable and empirical world that we can see and measure, which is why his arm is outstretched with his palm down to the ground, toward the material world. This is, of course, a major reduction of their work and thinking, but it helps us to contextualize and understand the primary difference between these two thinkers. It also helps us to understand how their legacies are still alive in contemporary disciplines. In universities, we still have a great divide between the humanities and the sciences.*

One of the first lessons in an American "college composition" or first-year writing course covers Aristotle's persuasive appeals of *ethos, pathos,* and *logos.* In Aristotle's terminology, these are the artistic proofs. They must be invented by the speaker (or writer, advertiser, politician, etc.) to embellish an argument and to persuade an audience. These were set up by Aristotle in contrast to what he called inartistic proofs, or the raw facts of a matter. I want to provide some examples to explain the artistic proofs of ethos, pathos, and logos.

Perhaps the most powerful of the artistic proofs, according to Aristotle, was ethos. Where all else fails, humans tend to look toward speakers who they think are credible to find their information. We trust a physician because they have a medical degree and wear a white lab coat—they look and speak like a doctor, so they must know what they're talking about. This is ethos. In contemporary English, ethos roughly translates to character or credibility. Ethos, as an artistic proof, is an appeal to a person's good name. A simple example to help us understand this would be to consider how modern political advertisements attempt to discredit opposing candidates by calling attention to their apparent personal defects or past mistakes—sometimes called "attack ads." By attempting to discredit the opponent, an attack advertisement can diminish the *ethos* of a candidate, leading us to lose trust in their words. The effect is akin to the Scooby-Doo gang pulling the mask off the goblin. It wasn't a monster at all! It was just Old Mr. Jenkins the whole time. Once the mask has been lifted, the spellbinding power of persuasion loses its effect.

Ethos creeps into almost every moment of our waking lives. When we trust the words of a medical doctor, it is because we have been persuaded by their credibility. We trust them because of almost countless effects that constitute their character: their medical degree and education; their style of speech, which is rich with scientific and technical terminology; their confident mannerisms; the white coat; the very name of "doctor," which instills in us a sort of reverence for their profession, and thus, their opinion. There is nothing inherently malicious in this unless the powers of ethos are used for the wrong reasons. We are, generally speaking, smart in trusting a medical doctor to provide us with a proper diagnosis and treatment options. That is their specialty, and they are credible. If they come across a problem outside their domain of knowledge and expertise, then the medical doctor will consult with a colleague and reference the relevant medical literature to attempt to solve the problem. We have every reason to trust a doctor, but we should understand all the mechanisms that lead us to do so.

The same effect occurs with politicians, business leaders, and government officials, as well as others in positions of power and authority. Herein, we begin to see problems arise. There is no reason why any random politician is an expert in renewable-energy science, military strategy, transportation logistics, emergent technologies, economics, or any of the other pressing matters upon which they vote and create legislation. In fact, we're lucky if a politician even has a law degree—according to the Congressional Research Service, only one third of United States House of Representatives members have a law degree, and only half of US Senators have a law degree. At the time of the study, only four US Senators had a medical degree and only four US Senators had a doctoral degree of another kind, such as a PhD. The people who are making complex decisions about the policies that govern the way we live are *not* experts in the areas on which they are voting and legislating. And these are, often, issues that strike to the heart of the very future of our planet and our species, if we think about the potential calamities of nuclear war, international relations, global climate change, and other large-scale global existential issues such as funding space travel, preservation of animal species, and so on. Yet, these are our representatives. Why did we vote for them? What other options did we have? How did they persuade us to believe that they were in any way qualified to help govern our world in distress, when so many people need help just surviving, buying or growing food, and paying rent? What sane society gives clowns the keys to its country?

Aristotle explains that when all else fails, ethos is the most powerful of the persuasive appeals. Politicians weave stories and build narratives to explain their credibility in decision-making and leadership. They wear sharp suits and ties, and project authority with the body and the voice. They use media—both traditional outlets like television and radio as well as digital media like Twitter, Instagram, Facebook, YouTube, Google, and disguised advertising known as native advertising—to control the perception of their image. We come to trust the figures of our government because of the very image of credibility that they create. In short, it is mostly smoke and mirrors. We have been persuaded to allow unqualified individuals to make extraordinary decisions that affect our daily lives and the future of our species—the very future of humanity.

How else are we persuaded? Aristotle goes on to explain the role of pathos, another of the three artistic proofs. Humans are very social and emotional creatures, and our hearts are easily stirred. Pathos is the appeal to emotions. We see it rampant in advertising but also throughout the political sphere. Communications play on our desires, our fears, our hopes, and our dreams. Sometimes, advertising is much baser than this—I remember a shockingly stupid television advertisement for a major fast food chain with a fit, lean, young, blonde woman biting into a massive hamburger with big, bold, heavily distorted rock and roll power chords as the music bed. And that was essentially the entire advertisement. We are easily misled by our emotions. Philip Taylor, my favorite propaganda historian, explains how military leaders and warlords have been using speeches to rouse their troops for thousands of years—this certainly predates ancient Greece, even, and is almost as old as war itself. Shakespeare dramatizes such an emotional, rousing, military speech in the moments leading up to the Battle of Agincourt on St. Crispin's Day, something that we might imagine has been taking place throughout human history:

> Familiar in his mouth as household words
> Harry the king, Bedford and Exeter,
> Warwick and Talbot, Salisbury and Gloucester,
> Be in their flowing cups freshly remember'd.
> This story shall the good man teach his son;
> And Crispin Crispian shall ne'er go by,
> From this day to the ending of the world,
> But we in it shall be remember'd;
> We few, we happy few, we band of brothers;
> For he to-day that sheds his blood with me
> Shall be my brother; be he ne'er so vile,
> This day shall gentle his condition:
> And gentlemen in England now a-bed

Shall think themselves accursed they were not here,
And hold their manhoods cheap whiles any speaks
That fought with us upon Saint Crispin's day.[71]

And later, during the battle, the famous lines:

Once more unto the breach, dear friends, once more;
Or close the wall up with our English dead.[72]

The power of language and the power of the human voice is so strong that it can influence people to take up swords against their neighbors and sacrifice their lives to the arbitrary boundaries of a mostly imaginary nation. We can be persuaded to buy things, to vote particular ways, even to think certain ways and to change our values if we allow ourselves to be susceptible and if we do not question the onslaught of communication coming at us.

I suppose I am just as guilty as anyone else of being persuaded, even though I study persuasion and rhetoric. I was studying English at Roosevelt University in downtown Chicago in 2008 when Barack Obama was elected president. On November 4, election night, a massive surge of people flooded to Grant Park to see Obama speak. The energy was electric. We all had visions of "HOPE" in our minds—that nebulous propaganda slogan—and probably, we earnestly believed that some massive change was coming: that the working class would finally be rewarded, that housing would become affordable, that wages would go up. The "HOPE" slogan was printed on a highly stylized campaign poster that spread like wildfire to t-shirts and Facebook like wildfire. It was all over the place. I remember the excitement I felt; it was captured by a European photographer while

I sat on a hill —I am probably in a magazine or newspaper somewhere from that night. I even bought a t-shirt from a street vendor. We were all swept away by language, image, voice, and visuals. All who were there had been worked over completely. We were persuaded to vote for and *feel* something about this man, Obama.

The political reality was that not much changed for the average working-class American in the following years. Sure, some things happened. But fifteen years later, houses are still not affordable, there is still no universal healthcare, wages have been mostly stagnant, and little progress has been made in improving quality of life for most Americans. Yet, we wanted to believe, especially in that moment of fervor and rally. That is the power of emotion and pathos in persuasion.

Logos is the final of Aristotle's artistic proofs, and it helps to explain the underlying logic of advertisements. Particularly, Aristotle explains in *Rhetoric* the function of the enthymeme, which is a type of truncated syllogism. That probably sounds like nonsense, but you'll likely see the enthymeme appearing in all sorts of advertisements after you've gotten a sense of it. A syllogism, first, is a type of logical construction that is just like the transitive property of equality in mathematics: if $A=B$ and $B=C$, then $A=C$. The most famous example of the syllogism is:

Proposition 1: Socrates is a man. ($A=B$)
Proposition 2: All men are mortal. ($B=C$)
Conclusion: Therefore, Socrates is mortal. ($A=C$)

This is a classic syllogism. Now, an enthymeme is simply a syllogism where one of the propositions or the conclusion is missing. The audience is left to "fill in the gaps," and conclude on their own. Imagine, for example, an advertisement for a fossil fuel company. The television or YouTube video advertisement might say something like:

Proposition 1: Fossil Fuels Inc. cares about the environment.

Proposition 2: You care about the environment, too.

Conclusion: [Therefore, you should come to our gas stations because we care more about the environment than our competitors, and you don't want the world to end, do you?]

In the above construction, the conclusion is missing. As viewers or readers, we don't want to be absolutely hit over the head by an advertisement. We might call this a "ham-handed" advertisement. Now, the propositions here might not be true. We have no idea if Fossil Fuel Inc. cares about the environment any more than their competitor, Big Fossil Co. But they can get away with saying that in an advertisement any day of the week, and they certainly do.

More interestingly, perhaps, is that one or more of the propositions might not be stated directly in language. Instead, for Proposition 2 of the above example of an enthymeme, we might imagine that a visual plays where polar bears are standing sadly on sheets of ice floating away into the ocean. But this visual content could be used for any number of reasons; it could be followed by a call to action asking for us to vote for a particular politician who will advocate for climate-change reform and save the polar bears. Or, just as easily, such a striking visual could be used by a major oil company to attempt to persuade us of their commitment to the environment. This has the same function. It makes us care. It makes the argument for us, so much so, that we barely have to think. This is the power of logos. Whether these logical structures are learned or intrinsic is still up for debate; Piaget conducted many studies which marked the milestones of important logical developmental abilities in children, but it's still not clear precisely where they come from. Either way, they are inside of us for advertisers, governments, organizations, and individuals to prey upon. And we best watch out.

For Aristotle, logos can also mean the argument itself. That is, did the speaker progress through his or her points in a logical fashion, and did all these claims come together to make a convincing speech? Aristotle warns us—especially in another work, his important *Politics*—that the art of speech can be used for malicious purposes, after all, just like Plato recognized. Sometimes we are tricked into thinking a speech has a logical progression when really it relies on one or more logical fallacies. A logical fallacy is incorrect reasoning that appears to make sense, but does not hold up when investigated more closely (for some live examples, just watch one of the editorial segments on a major cable news network for a couple of minutes and you can practically play Logical Fallacy Bingo). Fallacies are common errors that undermine the logic of an argument, but they can also be used to trick, mislead, and disinform.

## COMMON LOGICAL FALLACIES

If we learn to spot common logical fallacies, we can better protect ourselves from persuasive, malevolent speakers. A logical fallacy is sometimes fallacious because the propositions are untrue or something in the content of the argument is incorrect (informal fallacy), and sometimes because of an il-logical construction or the very form of the argument (formal fallacy).

Sometimes a speaker, advertisement, or other media might use a logical fallacy by mistake. But this is really no excuse. Whether a logical fallacy is used intentionally or mistakenly, it is unethical. We are responsible for our own words in the world, and we must carefully cultivate them. In our list of log-ical fallacies, here, I will use the term "speaker," but I am just using it in a general sense. We can see logical fallacies in many places, including political speeches, local advertisements, bill-boards, social media, books, and often, in use by large corpo-rate-American news stations. This is especially true of their editorial segments, but the fallacies also appear in general re-porting and broadcasting. Keep an eye out for logical fallacies everywhere—not just in formal, spoken speeches, but in writ-ing, audio, video, websites, and social and digital media too.

MOVING THE GOALPOSTS: The speaker changes the require-ments for the debate while it is still in progress. For example, Speaker A might ask, "Show me where that's documented in the medical literature!" to which Speaker B replies with the name of a solid, credible peer-reviewed journal article. Speaker A then says, "Fine, show me ten places where it's documented in the medical literature!" The goal has been moved. There's nothing wrong with asking for more evidence, but it's not a legitimate reason to undermine another person's argument (especially on the spot).

IF-BY-WHISKEY: Referring to an incomprehensible speech from 1952 by Noah S. "Soggy" Sweat Jr., a Mississippi lawmaker, an

"If-By-Whiskey" argument is one in which the speaker does not really take a stance, but instead equivocates and attempts to appeal to more than one side of an argument. See if you can understand why Sweat's speech (below) is problematic. The context is that Sweat is speaking on the subject of whether Mississippi should allow the sale of alcoholic beverages, or whether it should continue prohibition. Can we guess which way he will vote on the matter? See for yourself:

"My friends, I had not intended to discuss this controversial subject at this particular time. However, I want you to know that I do not shun controversy. On the contrary, I will take a stand on any issue at any time, regardless of how fraught with controversy it might be. You have asked me how I feel about whiskey. All right, here is how I feel about whiskey:

If when you say whiskey you mean the devil's brew, the poison scourge, the bloody monster, that defiles innocence, dethrones reason, destroys the home, creates misery and poverty, yea, literally takes the bread from the mouths of little children; if you mean the evil drink that topples the Christian man and woman from the pinnacle of righteous, gracious living into the bottomless pit of degradation, and despair, and shame and helplessness, and hopelessness, then certainly I am against it.

But, if when you say whiskey you mean the oil of conversation, the philosophic wine, the ale that is consumed when good fellows get together, that puts a song in their hearts and laughter on their lips, and the warm glow of contentment in their eyes; if you mean Christmas cheer; if you mean the stimulating drink that puts the spring in the old gentleman's step on a frosty, crispy morning; if you mean the drink which enables a man to magnify his joy, and his happiness, and to forget, if only for a little while, life's great tragedies, and heartaches, and sorrows; if you mean that drink, the sale of which pours into our treasuries untold millions of dollars, which are used to provide tender care for our little crippled children, our blind, our deaf, our dumb, our pitiful aged and infirm; to build highways and hospitals and schools, then certainly I am for it.

This is my stand. I will not retreat from it. I will not compromise. [73]

CHERRY-PICKING: Cherry-picking occurs when particular and specific studies or data points are used to prove a point, while ignoring all the other relevant data and analyses. An example would be if someone said, "Look, Hitler had dogs. He must not have been a bad person. An evil man could not have the heart to take care of his dogs like that. The dogs look perfectly happy." Hopefully you can spot the issue, here. We can't overlook all of the data and evidence. Adolf Hitler was responsible for the deaths of millions in WWII and the deaths of millions more in genocidal death and labor camps. The fact that he owned dogs is a cherry-picked piece of evidence. We often find people cherry-picking data and evidence intentionally, but we should also be careful to check our own arguments to make sure our own biases have not led us to cherry-pick our information. This is a common issue I see in freshman and sophomore level undergraduate essays and research papers; they will seek out facts and figures that support their opinions rather than look at the bigger picture to understand what the body of literature at large has to say on a matter.

ARGUMENT FROM REPETITION: The speaker repeats their points over and over until their opponent gives in, and then asserts that they must be correct because no one will challenge them on it. This is among the dirtier tricks employed by rhetorical bullies and the illogical. We see these types of immoral rhetorical techniques and logical fallacies used in political debates quite frequently, but they can also appear in advertising strategies. For example, sometimes advertisements are targeted at a specific population with high frequency and the advertiser deliberately overlooks oversaturation or burnout. If we repeat a lie enough times, people start to believe it. This is a dangerous precedent to set, and it can be used by anyone, including politicians, organizations, individuals, and massive corporations. Consider Thomas Smith's little poem from his 1885 work, Successful *Advertising:*

> *The first time people look at any given ad, they don't even see it.*
> *The second time, they don't notice it.*
> *The third time, they are aware that it is there.*
> *The fourth time, they have a fleeting sense that they've seen it somewhere before.*
> *The fifth time, they actually read the ad.*
> *The sixth time they thumb their nose at it.*
> *The seventh time, they start to get a little irritated with it.*
> *The eighth time, they start to think, "Here's that confounded ad again."*

*The ninth time, they start to wonder if they're missing out on something.*

*The tenth time, they ask their friends and neighbors if they've tried it.*

*The eleventh time, they wonder how the company is paying for all these ads.*

*The twelfth time, they start to think that it must be a good product.*

*The thirteenth time, they start to feel the product has value.*

*The fourteenth time, they start to remember wanting a product exactly like this for a long time.*

*The fifteenth time, they start to yearn for it because they can't afford to buy it.*

*The sixteenth time, they accept the fact that they will buy it sometime in the future.*

*The seventeenth time, they make a note to buy the product.*

*The eighteenth time, they curse their poverty for not allowing them to buy this terrific product.*

*The nineteenth time, they count their money very carefully.*

*The twentieth time prospects see the ad, they buy what it is offering.* [74]

Only a few decades later, Adolf Hitler would explain the Big Lie in his infamous work, *Mein Kampf*. A Big Lie is a massive distortion of the truth so epic in proportion that no one could possibly question it, such as blaming Germany's economic woes on the Jewish population, or alleging that climate change is a liberal hoax, or that the coronavirus vaccination was a plot by

Microsoft to inject tracking chips into US citizens. The trained rhetorician—and now you, my dear readers—will be prepared to stand up and fight for the truth. We know that insisting on something repeatedly does not make it true.

RED HERRINGS: The Red Herrings are an entire class of logical fallacies which explain the strategy of redirecting the subject of a conversation. We make this mistake all the time in our interpersonal relationships: "Maybe I didn't wash the dishes, but you forgot to pay the electric bill last month! Why should I take care of the house when you can't even remember the bills?" Red herrings are distractions that change the direction of the argument or debate and distract listeners from the primary subject and themes. Red herrings are also an important tool in propaganda and war communication. A recent example is how Russian leader Vladimir Putin labeled the Ukrainians "neo-Nazis" in attempt to justify the Russian invasion of Ukraine. This is not only factually incorrect but serves as a distraction and redirection of the truth. Red herrings can be used at a smaller scale as well. Someone might use the "Poison the Well" logical fallacy, a specific type of *ad hominem* logical fallacy, to attempt to discredit another speaker. For example, Speaker A might say to Speaker B, "What you say certainly can't be true. How can we trust someone who has so recently been divorced and is now unstable? Should we trust someone to make legislative decisions who cannot even keep his family together?" An *ad hominem* attack (literally Latin for "against the person") is directed at the person instead of the argument.

ARGUMENTUM AD POPULUM: The *argument ad populum* is also called the "bandwagon argument," and it is a broad appeal to the public that is erroneous. In short, it's the argument that states: "Everyone is doing it!" We see this used in interpersonal communication in peer pressure situations, but we also see it at the global scale when massive corporations use this tactic in their advertising strategies (especially to stoke FOMO, or the "Fear of Missing Out"). But this fallacy is also often used in speeches, texts, debates, and other media: "The majority of Americans believe X to be true. Why don't you?" There's no evidence to substantiate the claim, and even if it were true and supported by data from a massive poll or survey, we should remember that large populations can be absolutely incorrect about their positions on the truth. Consider how most ancient Greeks believed that ritual sacrifice would appease the gods, or how there was massive support for Germany's Nazi party in the 1930s and 1940s.

THE STRAWMAN: The Strawman Fallacy occurs when someone deliberately misrepresents the argument of another person. Speaker A has a reasonable request and asks, "Can you please wash the dishes for me tonight? I had a hard day and I need to get the laundry going right now and put the kids down to sleep." Speaker B resorts to a Strawman Fallacy and says, "Oh, so you want me to just do *everything* around the house, now? You think I've just got all the time in the world on my hands, don't you?"

Now, these are just a handful of the many types of logical fallacies that surround us. There are hundreds of documented logical fallacies that explain how we may think erroneously about the world—and by that nature, just as many formal ways for us to be tricked into believing someone else's perspective. And that's ultimately what this all comes down to. Persuasion is the art of trying to get someone to change their beliefs, perspectives, or choices. As the American rhetorician Lloyd Bitzer put in his famous 1968 essay, "The Rhetorical Situation," rhetoric is a mode of altering reality. Persuasive language can literally change the way we perceive and think about the world. It can influence the way we spend our money, spend our time, or who we vote into office. And the effects then ripple out through history and time and have material consequences. Language changes the world. And do we want the world to be changed based on truthful language or false language? If we seek for the truth, then we must be vigilant in detecting logical fallacies and cutting through persuasive speech that is persuasive for the wrong reasons.

Aristotle defined rhetoric as "the faculty of observing in any given case the available means of persuasion." The rhetorician is someone who can see and understand what will be persuasive in each context, based on the audience, the available arguments, and the situation at hand. Plato went so far as to say that we must understand the "soul" of our audience, and that we must match our speech to the type of soul of the listener. It's hard not to think of the Cambridge Analytica scandal and the modern practice of psychographics in this context. The 2019 film *The Great Hack* directed by Amer and Noujaim details how the UK-based propaganda firm Cambridge Analytica illegally scraped data from Facebook users' profiles to create advertisements that were based on the five-factor OCEAN personality model. OCEAN is a five-part personality model that is used in the field of psychology to describe human dispositions and behavioral tendencies. O=Openness, C=Conscientiousness,

E=Extroversion, A=Agreeableness, and N=Neuroticism. These traits can be mapped to peoples' voting tendencies. For example, people who score high in trait "Openness" (the willingness to try new things and their receptivity to new information and ideas) can be used as a general predictor for someone's willingness to vote for a more progressive or liberal candidate, while people who are low in trait "Openness" are more likely to vote for conservative candidates. While this a bit reductive, there is common sense in it—people who are more likely to be open to new ideas would gravitate towards a "progressive" or change-oriented political ideology, while those who are less open to new ideas are more likely to be politically conservative. These are classical definitions of liberalism and conservatism—one party that wants to shake things up and see how we can make the world better, and one party that likes things the way they are and doesn't want to change. In a nutshell, to want to "conserve" the past is to be conservative, while to look toward "progress" is to be progressive.

Cambridge Analytica worked for Donald Trump's presidential campaign in 2016. Through their data, they identified the profiles of individuals who were "on the fence" about which presidential candidate they would vote for in the upcoming US election, and they bombarded those "persuadable" individuals with advertisements, including doctored, edited images and videos showing Hilary Clinton in handcuffs (though Hilary Clinton has never been found guilty of any of the many allegations against her). In this sense, modern digital advertisers can follow Plato's formula of literally matching their messaging to the "soul" of the social media user—that is, they can create messaging that is specifically targeted at people with particular personalities and then develop creative content that will work them over most effectively. This same practice is conducted by most US businesses when they use data within Facebook's Advertising Manager to direct their advertisements at specific populations with specific incomes, education levels, behaviors, and interests.

For Aristotle, rhetoric was a neutral art that could be used for good or evil. Rhetoric is also a set of tools that can help us make sense of the frighteningly persuasive messages that are sent to us all the time. We like to think of ourselves as rational, smart, logical creatures who don't make mistakes and would never be fooled by these simple party tricks. We say, "sure, maybe other people are convinced by advertising and disinformation campaigns, but not me." I have no doubt that you are intelligent, but I would ask you to remember that the global advertising spend estimates are in excess of $700 billion annually, with the largest portion of that going to digital advertising, such as YouTube pre-roll videos and targeted Twitter, Instagram, and Facebook advertisements, as well as search engine placement advertisements on Google. If it didn't work, people would not pay $700 billion to run these advertisements. I sometimes encourage my students to "follow the money" to learn more about the origin and intents of an issue. We might do the same here. If in doubt, follow the money. Like Quintilian said, money can be quite persuasive.

Armed with our understanding of the systems of rhetoric through the ancient Greeks, we might now venture forward in time to the Romans, and then the nineteenth, twentieth, and twenty-first centuries to seek to understand what "harvest" we have yielded from our societies. Has truth reigned supreme, or has falsehood prevailed? How have mass media technologies such as the telephone and radio shaped persuasion and disinformation? And how have our new computer technologies and the ubiquitous smartphone again changed the landscape with their hyper-targeted, weaponized information? At least now, we are well armed with some tools which might protect us from demagogues and liars. From Aristotle, we have the artistic proofs of ethos, pathos, and logos, a bit of logic and a keen eye for logical fallacies, and a recognition of the importance of audience and the form of a speech. From Plato we have an understanding that rhetoric must be coupled with philosophy if we would like to ever get to the "truth" of a matter. And I have endeavored to demonstrate that the truth is a tricky thing to catch—but that makes it even more worthwhile to seek. If nothing else, rhetoric can help us better understand when we are being lied to and gives us the power to dismantle fallacious and erroneous arguments when they are being tossed at us. The art of rhetoric gives us the courage to stop and think, and to think for ourselves. Thinking is the one thing the ruling class would prefer you not to do. Thinking is dangerous, after all. From the ancient kings of old, to the present-day Silicon Valley technology companies, we are always being asked to fall in line, be quiet, and keep our heads down. Understanding rhetoric gives you permission to step out of line, let your voice be heard, and raise your head toward finding the truth. Let's take our rhetoric and our philosophy with us as we move forward.

*Figure 8: Photograph of a Contemporary Ford Truck*[75]

# How to Conduct Rhetorical Analysis of Media

## A Sample Analysis of an Advertisement

| Category | What to Look For | Observations | Analysis |
| --- | --- | --- | --- |
| Media | What is the form and medium of the information? We might look for: genre, text, editing, motion, color, symbolism, music, and other elements. How is the media edited and constructed, and for what purpose? | The advertisement is in the form of a thirty-five-second YouTube video with music and narration. There are fast cuts. The ad might be served as a YouTube pre-roll advertisement or television advertisement, or even on social media, as video ads can be served on many different media platforms. The music bed is subdued but sounds like an acoustic guitar strumming, perhaps to evoke a "country" aesthetic. The narrator/voice actor is male, perhaps in his thirties, with a slight Midwestern American accent. | The advertisement is clearly designed to make you desire the Ford F-150 truck. Social media users are up to 3x more likely to click on a video advertisement compared to a static image. The acoustic music bed plays into the country, rural, rustic vibe of the advertisement, while the setting and timbre of the narrator's voice, seems to target those who want to associate with the American working class, rural lifestyle, or those who identify with that group. |
| Ethos | What appeals to *ethos* are evident in the media or information? *Ethos* is the rhetorical appeal of credibility. In other words, what is the general character or quality of the speaker or media, or how does it attempt to build its credibility with the audience? | Ford is a mostly American automobile manufacturer and a household name. I feel like I can mostly As such, you may feel you can trust this company, but you should research more about them and see if the associations you have with this company are actually true. The *ethos* of the video could be described as rustic, rural, tough, strong, and hard-working, even as evidenced by the diction choices in the narration. | There is nothing inherently rustic, hard-working, or rural/country about a truck, and Ford is using this characterization (*ethos*) to play into your desire to associate and identify with the rural, rustic, hard-working American identity. The Ford company wants you to believe that it is associated with, and is supported by, middle-class and working-class Americans and the virtue of hard work. |

| Pathos | What are the appeals to *pathos* evident in the media or information? *Pathos* is the rhetorical appeal of emotion. In other words, how does this media play with your feelings or try to make you feel a certain way? | The video plays with many emotions. You may feel jealous of others who can afford this vehicle (and thus feel anger or sadness), which is why such an advertisement might show payment plan or financing options. Strong language like "tough" and "smart" are personal traits that perhaps you want to aspire to or feel deficient in. The video may be described as country, rural, rustic, nostalgic, homegrown, small town. This may play on your memories and sense of identity and even your pride and nationalism. It may make you feel homesick, nostalgic, or desirous. | The video wants you to identify with the object (the truck), the person driving it, and its overall image. The advertisement may make you feel jealous, nostalgic, aspirational, or desirous so that you will be more likely to purchase this vehicle and think about this vehicle. The video may want you to identify with the people in the video. "I want to be like that man—smart, tough, American, proud, hard-working—so I will buy this truck to become like him." |
| --- | --- | --- | --- |
| Logos | What are the appeals to *logos* evident in the media or information? *Logos* is the appeal to logic. Does the information appeal to your rational sensibilities? What are the arguments it attempts to make? | The video uses many technical descriptions to entice you to buy the vehicle: "3,325 Pounds of Payload" and "3.5L Powerboost Full Hybrid Powertrain" and "7.2KW of Exportable Power." It sounds impressive but some of this is obvious technical marketing. "Powerboost" doesn't really mean anything. There is also an underlying logic of the advertisement in the form of an enthymeme: "If you buy this truck, then you will be smart, tough, and American." | The appeals to *logos* balance out the emotional appeals by showing the "smart" features of the vehicle which make the vehicle appear impressive in relation to competing trucks and automobiles. The technical specifications may or may not be useful to you. You would need to research further and determine your needs as a consumer. The underlying logic is obviously disinformation: Buying this truck will not make you smarter, tougher, or any more American than you already are or are not. |

| Disinformation | Does the information lie or bend the truth? If so, it may be disinformation or contain elements like disinformation. | The central argument of the video seems to be "If I buy a Ford F-150 truck, then I will be tough, strong, and smart." You can generally trust the technical information, such as technical specifications about the vehicle, as many companies try to abide by advertising regulations. However, You understand you might be unfamiliar with these regulations, and unless you're an engineer or mechanic, you may not have the technical expertise to understand these specifications. They are still a form of "technical marketing." The video is loaded with *pathos* and strong uses of language, imagery, and music, which may be misleading and intentionally persuasive, and are similar to many forms of disinformation. | The central argument of the video is clearly a lie. The purchase of a truck cannot change a person's strength or personal qualities or transform them significantly. The purchase of a vehicle should be done carefully and is an important financial and personal decision. This is obviously an advertisement, but functions at a similar level as disinformation by lying to me. Purchasing this truck will not make anyone smarter, tougher, or stronger. The advertisement is similar to disinformation because it distorts reality and is explicitly persuasive rather than objective and neutral. Most people would dismiss this as only an advertisement, but it has definitive characteristics of disinformation and propaganda. |

BUT MONEY, LIKEWISE HAS THE POWER OF
PERSUASION, AS DO INTEREST, AND THE AUTHORITY
AND DIGNITY OF A SPEAKER, AND EVEN HIS VERY
LOOKS...

—QUINTILIAN [76]

# CHAPTER VII

# The Roman Rhetoricians: Rhetoric and Everyday Life

*A liar must have a good memory.*
—QUINTILIAN[77]

The ancient Romans were great borrowers from the ancient Greeks. They studied, adapted, and transformed for their own purposes the customs, gods, political institutions, art, manners, and intellectual traditions of the ancient Greeks. Ancient Rome faced many crises as it transitioned from republic to dictatorship to empire under Julius Caesar. Ancient Rome faced endless invasions from northern peoples and many tumultuous shifts in power over its two thousand-year history. From the early foundations of the Roman Republic around 509 BCE to the Fall of Constantinople in 1453 CE, the Romans had a long run. And rhetoric was a central institution of the Roman intellectual and civic life; it was embedded in Rome's educational institutions and inspired by thinkers like Plato and Aristotle. The Roman emperor Constantine would eventually move the seat of the empire from Rome in the west, to Constantinople, the city he founded in the east. Soon after, Christianity would become the most widespread religion in the empire. The King James Bible, in Ezekial 18, says, "The son will not share the guilt of the father, nor will the father share the guilt of the son. The righteousness of the righteous man will be credited to him, and the wickedness of the wicked will be charged against him." [78] True to form, the ancient Romans learned many lessons from the ancient Greeks but faced extraordinary troubles of their own making.

There's much we can still learn from the qualities of the Roman rhetoricians and the conditions under which they lived; this is especially true of two of Rome's greatest rhetoricians and thinkers, Cicero and Quintilian. The Roman statesman Cicero was said to have been such a powerful speaker and rhetorician that after his death, Marc Antony's wife Fulvia pulled the tongue from his decapitated head and, in furious vengeance, stabbed it over and over with a hair pin. Quintilian, later, laid down a program of prescription for teaching rhetoric to Roman citizens to ensure they would become useful political thinkers and speakers in the great machinery of the empire. And later still, St. Augustine attempted to reconcile Christianity with Greek and Roman philosophy and rhetoric. He introduced his own struggles into the intellectual stew before his death at the Siege of Hippo, where invading Germanic Vandals destroyed all but the city's cathedral and library. Eventually, after much contention, Christianity became commonplace in Rome, and citizens largely placed the problem of truth in the hands of God. All in all, these were strange and violent times, though the same could be said of other ancient civilizations, our own times, and in all likelihood, future times. Humans have a hard go of things.

# INVENTION: WHERE DO ARGUMENTS COME FROM?

The Roman rhetorician Cicero wanted very badly to continue the work of Plato but never seemed to face head on the central themes of *Phaedrus* and the looming problem of truth. Cicero valued truth and duty—perhaps more as an expression of citizenship to the growing Roman machinery than as the highest goal of an orator. Quintilian would later give us the idea of the ideal orator as "a good man speaking well," a formula we can use to assess credibility.

Cicero worked more clearly in the Aristotelean tradition of systematizing and categorizing frameworks of rhetoric. One of the most important legacies of Cicero as a rhetorician is his *De Inventione,* wherein he outlines the Five Canons of Rhetoric:

INVENTION
ARRANGEMENT
STYLE
MEMORY
DELIVERY

Invention is the process by which we develop our arguments and the contents of our writing and speeches. Where do ideas come from? You can't just wait around for inspiration to strike you. We must actively seek out lines of argumentation and test their validity. To help aid in invention, we use the *topoi* (simply "topics"), which are universal attributes of any subject.[79] Some examples of topoi include questions like:

- What is it made out of? What is its substance, material, or abstract?
- Where did it come from? What are its origins?
- What is it similar or dissimilar to? How can it be categorized?
- Does it exist or not exist? To what degree?
- Can it be quantified? How many or how much?
- What are the causes and effects of it?
- How long has it existed? What attributes of time does it have?
- Is it feasible?
- Is it desirable? What benefits or problems would it cause?
- Can it change? In what ways?

These are universal questions about a topic that can be applied to any subject to help us better understand it. For example, if you are asked to deliver a presentation about a water bottle, you could start by running this topic through the above topoi to attempt to better understand the object and to discover arguments about it.

Substance: It is made of plastic, which could have some environmental considerations or health effects. Origins: It was manufactured in China—I wonder what the conditions of the workers are like in the factory that produced this water bottle.

Similarity/Dissimilarity: It is like other vessels, perhaps there is an intriguing history of water bottles, canteens, and thermoses that could be explored. That relates to the element of time, as well—perhaps humans have been using water bottle-like objects for thousands of years.

Existence: Does it exist? Well, it seems to exist, and I have one here in front of me, but I wonder what percentage of Americans own a water bottle, and whether that has an impact on public health and dehydration statistics.

Quantity: How many water bottles are there in the United States? Is there a shortage or an overabundance? Do more need to be produced, or do they contribute to waste?

You get the idea. You can use the *topoi* to help grasp an understanding of any subject. The very trivial object that we focused on—the plastic water bottle that is found in most households—holds a vast number of mysteries and questions that only come to light when probed. A trained rhetorician is always asking questions about the possible arguments that can be invented about a subject as a means to explore its importance, relevance, and validity. Of course, you could film an eight-part documentary series about water bottles and their impact on human history—I'm not sure if anyone would be interested in it. You could begin research for a whole book about the history of the water bottle just based on the questions we asked above.

But the importance of invention becomes clear when we begin to apply it to the political sphere. We can ask these same questions about an issue that is raised in a political debate, such as questions asked in the 2020 US presidential debates between Trump and Biden. During the first debate, held on Tuesday, September 29, 2020 in Cleveland, Ohio, moderator Chris Wallace asked then-President Donald Trump and presidential candidate Joe Biden to explain their plan for dealing with the pandemic. Running the coronavirus as a subject through our *topoi*, we can ask serious questions that many people in the US disagree about: Does the pandemic exist, or not? Much disinformation was spread about the coronavirus being a "hoax," for example. Where did it come from? Some people believe the virus originated in a Chinese biological-weapons laboratory. Others say it came from human encroachment on nature, via a wet market. What is the virus similar or dissimilar to? An early wave of misinformation on social media showed people comparing the coronavirus to the flu in an attempt to downplay its severity. What is it made out of—what is its substance? This is hard to answer without a background in biology, virology, and infectious diseases, yet many people took to their mobile devices and keyboards to attempt to argue about the size of droplets and the effectiveness of mask mandates.

The *topoi*—or topics—can help us grapple with any subject by laying out for us the variety of arguments that can be composed—and disagreed on—by people. One of the great lessons of Invention is that arguments are not always constructed on good evidence, but are often based on values, perceptions, emotions, or other tenuous connections with reality. And we are easily persuaded when arguments are based on our values, perceptions, and emotions.

Let's examine the difference in rhetorical approaches by Biden and Trump as they answer the first question of the third presidential debate on October 22, 2020, at Belmont University in Nashville, Tennessee, moderated by Kristen Welker of NBC News: [80]

WELKER: And we will begin with the fight against the coronavirus. President Trump, the first question is for you. The country is heading into a dangerous new phase. More than forty thousand Americans are in the hospital tonight with COVID, including record numbers here in Tennessee. And since the two of you last shared a stage, sixteen thousand Americans have died from COVID. So please be specific: how would you lead the country during this next stage of the coronavirus crisis? Two minutes, un-interrupted.

TRUMP: So, as you know, 2.2 million people, modeled out, were expected to die. We closed up the greatest economy in the world in order to fight this horrible disease that came from China. It's a worldwide pandemic. It's all over the world. You see the spikes in Europe and many other places right now. If you notice, the mortality rate is down, 85 percent. The excess mortality rate is way down, and much lower than almost any other country. And we're fighting it, and we're fighting it hard. There is a spike. There was a spike in Florida, and it's now gone. There was a very big spike in Texas, it's now gone. There was a very big spike in Arizona, it's now gone. And there were some spikes and surges in other places. They will soon be gone. We have a vaccine that's coming, it's ready. It's going to be announced within weeks, and it's going to be delivered. We have Operation Warp Speed, which is the military, is going to distribute the vaccine. I can tell you from personal experience that I was in the hospital, I had it. And I got better, and I will tell you that I had something that they gave me—a therapeutic, I guess they would call it. Some people could say it was a cure. But I was in for a short period of time, and I got better very fast, or I wouldn't be here tonight. And now they say I'm immune. Whether it's four months or a lifetime, nobody's been able to say that, but I'm immune. More and more people are getting better. We have a problem that's a worldwide problem. This is a worldwide problem, but I've been congratulated by the heads of many countries on what we've been able to do with the—if you take a look at what we've done in terms of goggles and masks and gowns and everything else, and in particular, ventilators. We're now making ventilators. All over the world, thousands and thousands a month, distributing them all over the world, it will go away and as I say, we're rounding the turn, we're rounding the corner, it's going away.[81]

Here, Trump emphasizes the origins of the coronavirus to shift our attention away from the conditions in the United States. The origin of the virus is not particularly relevant to answering the question, yet it is used here by Trump to shift blame to another nation state: "this horrible disease that came from China." Next, Trump uses a rhetorical technique called **epistrophe,** which is repetition at the end of successive sentences, to emphasize a particular point. He says, "There was a spike in Florida, and it's now gone. There was a very big spike in Texas, it's now gone. There was a very big spike in Arizona, it's now gone." See the repetition at the end of the sentences in a parallel fashion: "it's now gone."

Yet, during this period, total daily global cases were rising steadily and had not yet peaked. Trump's argument that highly localized spikes had ended were not arguments that spoke to the greater truth that the pandemic was still an ongoing issue and reported cases were, in fact, rising. Trump goes on to test out a variety of techniques. He alludes to Operation Warp Speed thereby calling on the credibility of the military to deliver the vaccine; he gives an anecdote about how he has personally received the vaccine, which is a kind of identification strategy to attempt to show to an audience how similar he is to them—to allow the audience to identify with him. This is not an exhaustive analysis, but it provides a glimpse of the various techniques and lines of argument that are being made in response to a single question in a debate. Here, Trump is attempting to make the argument that he is the best candidate to handle the coronavirus response. Does he provide good evidence for that argument? You can decide.

Now, we see presidential candidate Joe Biden asked the same question:

WELKER: OK, former Vice President Biden, to you, how would you lead the country out of this crisis? You have two minutes uninterrupted.

BIDEN: 220,000 Americans dead. If you hear nothing else I say tonight, hear this. Anyone who's responsible for not taking control—in fact, not saying, I'm – I take no responsibility, initially—anyone who is responsible for that many deaths should not remain as President of the United States of America. We're in a situation where there are thousands of deaths a day, a thousand deaths a day. And there are over seventy thousand new cases per day. Compared to what's going on in Europe, as the New England Medical Journal said, they're starting from a very low rate. We're starting from a very high rate. The expectation is we'll have another two hundred thousand Americans dead by the time, between now and the end of the year. If we just wore these masks—the President's own advisors have told him—we could save one hundred thousand lives. And we're in a circumstance where the President, thus far, still has no plan. No comprehensive plan. What I would do is make sure we have everyone encouraged to wear a mask, all the time. I would make sure we move in the direction of rapid testing, investing in rapid testing. I would make sure that we set up national standards as to how to open up schools and open up businesses so they can be safe, and give them the wherewithal and financial resources to be able to do that. We're in a situation now where the New England Medical Journal—one of the serious, most serious journals in the whole world—said for the first time ever that this, the way this President has responded to this crisis, has been absolutely tragic. And so folks, I will take care of this, I will end this, I will make sure we have a plan. [82]

Here, Biden begins not by arguing that he is the best person to handle this job, but that the response so far has been highly problematic. He gives us an "inartistic proof," in Aristotle's terms—that is, he gives us facts or stats—about the seventy—thousand new cases per day. This is in sharp contrast to Trump's rhetoric about spikes being gone. Two very different perceptions of the same shared reality. Then, Biden attempts to make an appeal to logos—an appeal to our desire for data, science, and reason—by referencing the "New England Medical Journal," though he misspeaks the name of the journal, which is *The New England Journal of Medicine*. Biden then shifts his strategy to appeal to our pathos by showing how many more Americans might die if we do not change our course. Then, Biden begins to explain his own approach to handling the pandemic with a strong use of anaphora, or repetition at the beginning of parallel sentences: "What I would do is make sure we have everyone encouraged to wear a mask, all the time. I would make sure we move in the direction of rapid testing, investing in rapid testing. I would make sure that we set up national standards as to how to open up schools and open up businesses so they can be safe, and give them the wherewithal and financial resources to be able to do that." You can see the anaphora very clearly, which is here used to emphasize "I would make sure that..." to demonstrate the speaker's conviction and ability through repetition.

Cicero has left an important legacy for rhetoric, in my mind, as one who continued the early forms of technical rhetoric—the sorts of people who strove to develop systems of rhetoric, classify its characteristics, and make sense of how persuasion functions and how we can teach people to be better speakers. These Five Canons of Rhetoric remain a useful tool for thinking about both writing, as well as analyzing, content. You can analyze a speech or a textual or media object by running it through Cicero's Five Canons.

## QUINTILIAN THE EDUCATOR

One of the most striking lines from the Roman rhetorician Quintilian—sometimes called Quintilian the Educator—is his statement, "The mere look of a man can be persuasive." I think about this often, and indeed, in my classes, I often use clothing as a great example of practical, everyday rhetoric. We don't usually think of our clothing choices as rhetorical decisions, but aren't they? When you wear a suit and tie or a sharp, new dress to a job interview, you are doing so with a very particular purpose in mind: to impress upon the interviewer that you are a serious, professional, grown-up candidate, and that you will fit into the office culture. Or, say you are interviewing for a company that you know is much more laid-back, progressive, and hires younger creative types more often: you might go with your favorite flannel and some jeans to give off a young, hip, cool vibe. Take the scenario of a first date: you might spend an hour or more grooming, combing, selecting an outfit that's appropriate for the venue, but also has characteristics that flatter your body shape, or that express a particular part of your identity. And you don't show up to a heavy-metal rock show with khaki shorts and a polo shirt; you grab the black t-shirt with the heavy-metal band logo on it that you bought at a thrift store seven years ago, the one with the holes in it.

Of course, all of this is to say that looks can be persuasive, and we are making hundreds of strategic, rhetorical decisions every day. Whenever you write an email or send a text message, you are practicing the art of rhetoric. Imagine you go on that first date—you picked out a great outfit, felt confident, had fun, felt a connection, and things went well—so now you are wondering: what's next? Should you text them? Or would a phone call be better? Or are phone calls too formal—would a phone call make you look like a nerd? When should you call—should you wait a day, two days, a week? What if you wait too long—could you miss your chance to fall in love? Should you spill your guts and let them know you had a really great time and have feelings for them, or just play it cool and see where things go? These sound like silly, teenage questions, but they are all rhetorical questions, and important ones at that. Let's break it down a bit.

*Kairos* and *kronos* are ancient Greek terms related to timing. They are both in the lexicon of rhetoricians. Kairos is the opportune time, which we have talked about in another chapter. Kairos is when "the stars align," and everything happens at just the right time and right moment for a particular effect—and it's something that we can cultivate. For example, perhaps during your first date, your love interest mentioned that they have always wanted to see Peter Jackson's *The Lord of the Rings* films in the-aters, but they weren't interested in them at the time when they first came out, some twenty years ago, and only got into Tolkien's works when they were older. You just happen to have heard that a local, indie movie theater will be doing a showing of these films next week. So, you go buy the tickets and ask them out on a sec-ond date. During dinner, at just the right moment, when there's a casual pause in the conversation and there's a draft of romantic tension suspended in the air, you pull the tickets out of your pocket and tell them about your plans to take them to see the movie after dinner. That element of picking *just the right moment* is what kairos is all about.

Let's stick with our situation of the first and second date. The next question we must address is the one of *medium*. We asked: is it better to make a phone call, send a text message, or use social media to contact someone after a date? One hundred years ago, we might have asked whether it was better to ride to see them via horseback or to send a letter, and one hundred years from now young lovers will wonder how long of a three-dimensional ho-lographic message they should send. As famed media theorist Marshall McLuhan wrote: "The medium is the message."[83] What McLuhan meant by this is not far from what we're talking about—he mentions in interviews that the content of messaging is secondary, perhaps even incidental, when compared to the me-dium itself. In other words, it doesn't really matter *what* you are watching on the television in your living room. What matters is *that* you are watching television in your living room. It has al-ready occupied your living space, taken over your time, diverted your attention from everything else, and has taken a place in your life, restructuring the way you think and organize your ex-istence. Again: *the medium is the message.*

Today's media scholars recognize that both the content and the medium of the message are meaningful. Still, when we are wondering whether we should follow up from our first date using a phone call, a text message, or a social media message, we are asking questions about *medium*. The medium of the video game is deeply interactive and can tell extraordinarily engaging stories where people have a choice in the very way that the narrative plays out, making for engrossing storytelling and immersive experiences. Bibliophiles know the medium of the book intimately; they are in love with the feel of its weight in their hands, the very smell of the paper, the dust and age of the object, the softness of a fresh page and the sound that comes from turning that page, as they read cozily in their beds on a cold, wintry night or on the sands of a warm beach. Advertisers, too, know the power of medium, especially in their demographic sciences. When they want to reach a specific demographic via social media, they might choose LinkedIn over Facebook, or run a campaign on Reddit instead of Twitter. The decision will be based on their available data about the user bases and the specific profiles of who they want to target. The medium of a message has a way of working us over very effectively.

Consider the persuasiveness of a web page. The medium of the web page is very sneaky—we have been told time and time again throughout our lives: *do not trust everything you read on the Internet*. Yet, for some reason, there is a kind of apparent, intrinsic authority to anything that is published, anywhere, which simply spellbinds us humans. The thought process is subconscious, but it must go something like: "Well, I have read a lot of other things on the Internet that are probably credible and seemed correct, so this new thing I am reading must also be credible and correct. After all, who would just let someone put this up on the Internet if it weren't true? They can't just put anything online!" But, of course, anyone who knows anything about building and hosting websites will tell you that it's just a matter of a few clicks and twenty dollars and anyone can be running a blog within minutes, writing whatever they like. There's a beautiful, democratic freedom in that, and there's just as much a terror for the population who does not know how to decode and analyze the credibility of these sites. This is why we need rhetoric. We must evaluate the credibility of sources very carefully, because looking at the medium alone isn't enough. There is no single medium on Earth that is always 100 percent credible. You can't pick up any book in a library and say it is just as credible and well-vetted as another, just as you can't read a blog written by an anonymous user and say that it is just as credible as a Reuters news report.

All of this is merely to say that every day, we are making strategic, rhetorical choices. When you are thinking about how to communicate with someone after a date, you are thinking about timing; you are thinking about the medium; and we haven't even talked about one of the most crucial elements yet: the content. There is syntax to consider—the arrangement of the words—as well as diction—the choice of precisely which words you'll use. Will you use slang and emojis in a casual way to show that you're "in the know," or will that make you look desperate? Will you use one emoji, ironically, to strike a particular response? Will you be formal or casual? These are all rhetorical decisions that you make—usually without much conscious consideration. You rely on an intuitive, feeling-based process where you try to consider what the potential reaction will be from the reader/recipient.

The ancient Roman rhetoricians weren't much for emojis and texting (although their bathroom wall graffiti is worth reading, if you have a moment to find some translations on the web), but they were interested in the service of rhetoric to the state and the growing machinery and glory of Rome. Quintilian recognized that well-trained orators were vital for the functioning of a robust citizenry and spent countless hours training his students in the rhetorical arts. Roman students of rhetoric would have composed countless practice speeches to work out their arts—knowing the power that speech and language can have upon people, to persuade, to control, to move them to behave in particular ways. Roman rhetoricians understood, too, the power of speech to rouse troops, deal with enemies, and forge alliances—and for an ever-expanding Roman Empire, these were all tools that every military leader should have at his disposal.

One of the more fascinating pieces from Quintilian comes from one of his fictional legal case studies. He asks us to imagine a ritual sacrifice of a goat on a mountaintop or high plateau. The religious figure has gathered all the necessary tools and made their preparations for the sacrifice of the animal. They have their knife in hand. Naturally, they have brought a flute player with them to the top of the mountain to accompany the ritual sacrifice. Today, modes of music are still named after ancient Greek tribes. These modes were said to represent the temperament of various peoples outside of Athens—Lydian, Ionian, and so on (though the ancient Greek modes of music do not correspond to today's modes). The fittingness or rightness of music to a particular occasion was incredibly important to the ancient Greeks, and this insistence on fittingness carried over into ancient Roman cultural norms. In Quintilian's case study, he imagines that the flutist plays, accidentally, in the wrong mode, and the religious figure—knife in hand—is driven to such a madness that he hurls himself off the cliff, committing suicide. Quintilian then asks us to wonder: who is to blame, in this case? Can the flutist be tried for murder, and on what grounds? It's a fun thought experiment to begin with, but it also reveals much to us about how the ancient Romans thought about rhetoric, fittingness, persuasion, and music. What this shows us, is that to the ancient Romans, the powers of persuasion were enough to drive people to jump off cliffs. Indeed, the rhetorical machinery of ancient Rome—with no mass media as we think of it today—was powerful and persuasive enough to command and compel some of the most massive social, civil, and military organizations that have ever existed. The voice is a powerful tool.

But the ancient Romans—for all their love of Athens—never reached ancient Greece's heights of philosophical splendor. From all the lands of ancient Rome, there was no one to rival Socrates, Plato, or Aristotle. Or, if ever there were, their writings have not come down to us. Whether the philosophical spirit was crushed and purposefully eradicated in all the industry and statecraft of Roman bureaucracy, or whether such a state was not fertile ground for philosophical thought to develop, is hard to say—a chicken and egg question worthy of a dissertation or three. Which came first: the decline in philosophy, or the Roman imperial machinery? Did one lead to the other? To me, it seems like no unlikely coincidence. An empire whose system of education is intentionally designed to promote the development of loyal subjects to the Empire, will in turn create generation after generation of people who are loyal subjects to the Empire, and little more. Yet, that's not to say there weren't some great poets and thinkers to come out of this period—you can't stop everyone's soul from spilling over. I am reminded again of Faramir: "The Shire must truly be a great realm, Master Gamgee, where gardeners are held in high honor." Ancient Greece produced many philosophers. Ancient Rome far fewer.

## FLIPPING IT AROUND

Rhetoric, then, is a great tool for making speeches, controlling language, and even controlling populations and soldiers. But how does this help us with today's disinformation epidemic? This becomes readily apparent when we flip around the rhetorical toolkit. In the same sense that we can use rhetoric to craft effective messages, we can also use it to decode and analyze inbound messages, the kinds that come at us from billboards, television commercials, video games, political campaigns, speeches, films, and digital advertisements. The tools of rhetoric allow us to ask: What was the intent of the person who sent me this message? What did they want me to do and to think? Why did they formulate this message in this way, with this medium, in this language, with this particular design? And why did they send it at this particular time? These are the questions we can ask to unravel the secrets of the messages of the world around us and to better discern where the truth lies in the messaging, if there is any truth to be found there at all.

Some messages are blatant in their intentionality. We can look at WWII-era propaganda posters, now often parodied and remixed in popular culture, as simplistic case studies in rhetorical analysis. We read, "Loose lips sink ships!" and see a capsized ship plunging into the ocean. In reality, discussing the war with our neighbors will probably not start a chain of events leading to the sinking of an American vessel in the Atlantic. Then again, secrecy was of the utmost importance in the planning of the extraordinary invasion at Normandy that culminated in D-Day on June 6, 1944, an event that played into the Fall of Berlin the following spring when Allied troops and the Soviet Union together converged on the German capital. For causes like this, we can see why scholar Philip Taylor tells us that propaganda is ultimately a neutral art, and that we, at times, need the right kinds of propaganda, and more of it, in the world. It's interesting that one of the foremost experts on propaganda and its history would tell us that propaganda can aid us in profound ways—then again, consider such American propaganda campaigns that would lead to women's suffrage, child labor laws, or the creation of national parks—these are propaganda campaigns for good causes. Imagine a public health campaign that raises awareness about the benefits of brushing your teeth—it would be hard to find much fault in that. Propaganda is not inherently evil. Though my perspective as a rhetorician is less than enthusiastic about the prospect of even more propaganda in the world, whether for good or evil. I favor an idealistic vision of a world where each person is able to establish their own judgments without the aid of propaganda.

Most propaganda is more subtle. While The Stanford History Education Group study used a web page that was clearly marked, much propaganda and disinformation is veiled, obscured, and disguised. Take, for example, the very common form of advertising known as native advertising. The entire goal of native advertising is to disguise the advertisement to make it look as though it were organic, natural content. So, someone might write a piece that looks like an editorial or opinion article when really it is a paid promotion. Native advertising and content advertising are extremely common, and anyone spending even a few minutes on a contemporary social media site—whether it's Twitter, Instagram,

Facebook, or Reddit—will be exposed to hundreds of advertisements within just a few minutes of scrolling through the applica-
tion and browsing what they might think is organic content.

It's no wonder that the inquisitive and "pestering" nature of
someone like Socrates would be quickly snuffed out in ancient
Rome. We remember ancient Rome for many things, but it is not
for the quality and number of their philosophers. In comparison
to the Greeks, Rome's legacy includes very little original philosophical thought, though we do have some time-tested texts, like
Roman Emperor Marcus Aurelius's collected *Meditations*. The
well-oiled state of Rome was orderly, brutal, and militaristic in
its conquests and operations—characteristics which would help
the empire survive (at least in part) for nearly two thousand
years, until the Eastern Roman Empire fell as the walls of Constantinople were razed by massive cannons in 1453. Sophistry
and disinformation were almost essential parts of the Roman
mode of operation. There was little room for dissidents. And by
the time Christianity was in full force, "truth" for most ancient
Romans was outsourced to the divine, placed in the hands of
God, and the pursuits of science and philosophy were left behind.

...THE ART OF A SPEAKER WHO DOESN'T KNOW THE TRUTH AND CHASES OPINIONS INSTEAD IS LIKELY TO BE A RIDICULOUS THING—AND NOT AN ART AT ALL.

—PLATO [84]

## CHAPTER VIII

# Bogost in the Machine: Rhetoric and Digital Disinformation

*Everywhere we remain unfree and chained to technology, whether we passionately affirm or deny it. But we are delivered over to it in the worst possible way when we regard it as something neutral; for this conception of it, to which today we particularly like to pay homage, makes us utterly blind to the essence of technology.*
—MARTIN HEIDEGGER[85]

I like to reframe common knowledge in my college classrooms, so when discussing the power of language and oratory in a rhetoric course, I might say something deliberately unfamiliar, such as "Less than a hundred years ago, a genocidal maniac tried to take over the world. And both my grandparents fought against him." My students don't know quite what to think. "What are you talking about, Dr. Lawrence? This is real life." I like this approach, because it also surprises some of my undergraduates to realize just how connected we all are; they may have forgotten that their own grandparents or great-grandparents served in World War II. To understand that their professor's grandparents were veterans of that chapter of history creates a connective effect that at first surprises them. The story of Hitler, and his Minister of Propaganda, Joseph Goebbels, is a cautionary tale that can warn us of the awful power of rhetoric and the spellbinding effect of speech that concerned Plato. But it is a disservice, too, to minimize Hitler in this way.

We tend to think that Hitler's atrocities were the result of some dark, evil seed that must have sprung up in his very soul and corrupted his person. There must have been something wrong with him. But there was just as much wrong with the very social and economic fabric from which he emerged, and his evils could not have manifested without inspiration from people like Dietrich Eckart, who founded the predecessor to the Nazi party and even penned the Nazi's first anthem, the "Storming Song." There would have been no fiery Hitler speeches that rallied a nation without the inspiration of Italian Prime Minister Benito Mussolini whose exaggerated gestures and propaganda techniques influenced Hitler's style of delivery.

There could have been no Hitler without the emergence and misuse of so many new mass communication technologies. Wireless radios made their way into homes throughout the United States and Europe in the 1920s, and for the first time in human history, someone in power could simultaneously broadcast his message to millions of people. These technologies do not create disinformation but can facilitate its spread by a rapid multiplying and centralizing effect. It's not entirely surprising that Edward Gibbon spends a good amount of space in the beginning of his monumental *The History of the Decline and Fall of the*

*Roman Empire* telling us about the massive system of ancient Roman roads. [86] Without the (relatively) fast flow of communication enabled by this vast network of roadways, the ancient Romans likely would not have been able to maintain their stability for as long as they had. Of course, it all crumbled to bits over time, as all civilizations seem to do, but this technological system was the sort of glue that held the proverbial teacup together.

But wait: is a system of roads a form of technology? It's worth taking a step back and asking ourselves this question. The feminist scholar Donna Haraway plays with the boundaries of the term cyborg to invite us to question the extent to which technology is integrated in our lives and the role that it serves. [87] Haraway offers us some simple examples to chew on. Even our shoes are a type of technology because they augment the way that we interact with the world. For Haraway, it is impossible to escape technology, as we are always surrounded by it. Not just the shoes we are wearing but the truck that delivered the shoes to the store, the factories which produced the bricks from which the shoe store was built, the motherboard of the computer that is used in the store to maintain inventory, ad infinitum. Nearly everything we do and touch is enabled by technologies. Technologies are inventions that change the way we interact with the world. But technologies also change the way we think, feel, act, and perceive.

Martin Heidegger, with his neatly trimmed moustache, slicked-back hair, and focused gaze, looks equally to me like a nineteenth-century German philosopher as he does an over-stylized cartoon character. At his burial in 1976, Bernhard Welte remarked, "Why does Heidegger interest me? Once a whole world listened to him." His seminal work of philosophy, *Being and Time*, has been of great interest to me for more than twenty years, though I haven't quite gotten a reasonable sense of it, yet, and won't pretend to for the purpose of this book. I have focused, rather, on his oft-cited essay, "The Question Concerning Technology," published in 1954.[88] But Heidegger also interests me for other reasons.

Heidegger and his wife joined the Nazi Party in 1933, at the height of his career. His *Being and Time* was esteemed by his mentor, Husserl, and Martin Heidegger was appointed a rectorship. But the prestigious position lasted for only a year and a few months, and by 1934 Heidegger had resigned from his post and moved into a country cabin to escape the city life. As a professor who sometimes struggles to stay positive about his teaching load, I am often humored by the accounts of great writers and thinkers dealing with their own troubles with teaching. Heidegger was not alone in these struggles. Two other famous German philosophers, Ludwig Wittgenstein and Friedrich Nietzsche, had their own troubles with their students. Wittgenstein was placed in a rural elementary school in 1921 and wrote to Bertrand Russel of the "odiousness" of his work, describing his students as "good-for-nothing" and "irresponsible." Nietzsche, on the other hand, became a young professor of classics at the University of Basel at the age of twenty-four, but just ten years later, resigned from his position to travel Europe and work independently on his philosophy. I imagine if I could afford to retire to a cabin in the countryside, I would probably do the same thing at this point in my life.

I've found plenty of counterpoints to Heidegger's distaste for teaching. The theoretical physicist Richard Feynman explains in his rascally autobiography, *Surely You're Joking, Mr. Feynman!* how he never would have considered taking a job that didn't include some teaching. He remarks that he has seen how pure research positions have slowed others down, and how they get stuck with no new ideas coming at them. Teaching, on the other hand, forces one to continually review the fundamentals of one's field and to approach these fundamentals from new perspectives. And, most importantly, our students are always asking us interesting questions from "outside the box" of the discipline which may cause us to think about this fundamental knowledge from new perspectives. I often daydream about retiring early from teaching so that I can just work on my books and smoke cheap cigars in the sunshine, but I might have to agree with Feynman. This book, after all, is mostly the product of thinking through contemporary problems with disinformation in relation to the ancient Greek rhetoricians and philosophers who I have been reading, and teaching students about, for more than twenty years.

One semester, a particularly lively student who sat in the back of my Introduction to Rhetoric lecture in Swenson Hall at the University of Wisconsin – Superior campus asked, "Is time arbitrary?" We were reading Gerard Hauser's *Introduction to Rhetorical Theory* that semester, which I no longer use as a textbook for a variety of reasons. But in this book, Hauser explains how rhetoric arises in indeterminate spaces where there is not a straight, hard, scientific answer to a problem. For example, if we think of a question like, "Should the federal reserve raise interest rates?" there is no scientific formula for us to use to solve that problem. When we approach that problem, we must use an interdisciplinary approach from fields as diverse as economics, mathematics, sociology, ethics, business, and so on. And everyone who is asked that question will approach it with a very different set of beliefs, priorities, values, and ideologies. Beyond that, everyone who is asked that question will think about the question with a set of false beliefs, because all of us, excluding no one, have been tricked into believing something that isn't true at one point or another in our lives. We have *all* been subjected to disinformation at some point, and it has become part of our worldview.

Now, whether or not time is arbitrary is a fantastic question and would probably be better suited to a physicist than a rhetorician. There are some interesting answers to this question. Some of the ways that we keep track of time are completely arbitrary. For example, the days of the week (in English) are mostly derived from ancient Norse gods. Wednesday is named after Woden or Odin (Woden's Day), and Thursday for Thor (Thor's Day), which are interesting holdovers from the history of the English language. Then, of course, the fact that we use a seven-day system is not based in physical reality; it's a human creation. It's based roughly on the mistaken conception that seven is a sacred or spiritual number. But when we look at the month, we realize that the month is not entirely arbitrary. A month is roughly tied to the phases of the moon, which is a natural, observable, empirical phenomenon that would exist whether humans inhabited Earth or not. Then, the year is the clearest of the non-arbitrary ways we keep track of time. A year is just the amount of time that the earth takes to revolve around our nearby star, the sun (with some minor imperfections in the way that we keep track of it, involving leap years and all of that). And this is just one quick response to this question, based on how we keep track of time. Time does seem to be a dimension of our universe. Do other universes have time, or other sorts of time? We don't know right now. Anyway, I appreciate Feynman's perspective on teaching, because being asked questions keeps us on our toes, and helps us to think in new ways about things we think we know. A question I often get from students is, "What would Plato have

thought about x or y?" and while it's not very scholarly to con-
jecture or extrapolate in such a way, the question leads to some
fun thought problems.

Heidegger was certainly familiar with the ancient Greeks and
found inspiration in Aristotle's methods as Heidegger attempted
to understand the complex human relationship to technology.
Heidegger's "The Question Concerning Technology" fascinates
me; it's an essay that some of my students have even described as
"beautiful." In it, Heidegger urges us to question our relationship
to technology and to consider its effects on us. In classic Heideg-
gerian fashion, he asks us: what is the "essence" of technology?
He challenges us to move past an "instrumental" understanding
of technology. The "instrumental" theory of technology suggests
that technologies are tools that we use for our benefit. The purpose of a hammer is to use it for hammering nails. The purpose
of a cup of coffee is for delivering caffeinated beverages into our
mouths to make us feel more awake and do better work. But this
is too superficial an understanding of technology. The cup of coffee does more than just bring the coffee to our mouths—it enables an entire industry of coffee farmers. The coffee cup has
more nefarious implications and manifestations, as well. We can
think of an underpaid factory worker assisting with the mass
production of coffee cups, for example. The coffee cup is no mere
coffee cup. It is embedded in a network of effects that span the
entire globe, from the maritime workers who ship the beans to
the miners who work to extract the raw materials to create
smartphone components which you use to order the coffee cup
from an online retailer. In this immediate but nebulous way, technologies do not just *serve* humans; they influence and change the
way we behave, think, and act. Technologies work us over, as
much as we work them over.

Heidegger is very concerned with the dangers of technology. One can't help but wonder if the horrors of the second world war were looming in his mind. It's not unlikely that by 1954, the image of the Hiroshima and Nagasaki mushroom clouds would have been ubiquitous. Heidegger ultimately suggests that we must learn to master technology and understand our complicated relationship with it before it slips out of our control. It's not hard to see this process already happening When social media was first created, ostensibly, its purpose was to allow college kids to connect with each other, thereby making new friends online. Even if this was the original, honest intention of Facebook, it is now the world's largest advertising platform. It has morphed into a technology that is far outside of its original intended purpose and effects. Facebook utilizes powerful algorithms that are hidden to most users. We are constantly inundated with digital advertisements that attempt to coerce us to think, buy, and behave in certain ways. In many ways, as technology advances, it becomes harder and harder for us to grapple with it, control it, and understand it, and thus its influence over us grows.

In the 1920s throughout the United States and Europe, the rapid dissemination of wireless radio devices ushered in a new era of mass media propaganda and facilitated—or perhaps even created—the conditions under which oratory could be used to quickly persuade millions of listeners. Microphones, speakers, and amplification devices were also important technological inventions that allowed for large-scale rallies and political events like those we see documented in the infamous Nazi-era propaganda films, *The Victory of Faith* (1933) and *Triumph of the Will* (1935). [89] These films are accessible across the Internet on places like archive.org (the Internet Archive). I think, when possible, it is better to view these propaganda films in color so that we can better study the media in a way that is familiar to modern viewers.

The way the Nazi party used imagery, symbolism, architecture, flags, and icons to propagandize was not new. A golden eagle (*aquila*) was carried on a pole by a standard-bearer in every ancient Roman legion. The exact numbers of soldiers in the military fluctuated over ancient Rome's long and troubled history, but under Trajan there were between 360,000 to 380,000 infantry and cavalry, and this swelled to around five hundred thousand under the rule of Septimius Severus. A legion would have consisted of around 5,600 infantry and cavalry. Here, we have such an astounding example of how our history shapes our present. So much of the grand, martial posturing of ancient Rome still survives with us today in the parading and organization of contemporary military force. And as we have mentioned in earlier chapters, we have evidence as far back as Sargon I that architecture, iconography, and symbolism were used in wartime propaganda. What's particularly interesting is that these forms of propaganda were also used to indoctrinate civilian populations—not to inspire fear, but to inspire pride. Even today, in the United States, it's normal to see military equipment on display in local, rural Fourth of July parades. While more antiquated forms of propaganda and disinformation (such as iconography, architecture, and parades) are still apparent in our daily lives, the new forms of propaganda and disinformation are coming to us by way of our smartphones and in our everyday interactions with technology. Heidegger's warnings were prescient. While social media began with the instrumental purpose of connecting people, it is now a technology that is driving us further and further apart.

## THE DIGITAL SHIFT

One of the most interesting statistics that I've come across in my research related to fake news, propaganda, and digital media is that companies now spend more money on digital advertising than traditional advertising. That is, the total global digital advertising spend has now surpassed the total global traditional advertising spend. So, imagine every billboard, every piece of spam mail or print flyer, every television or radio commercial, every flashing neon sign, bus wrap, magazine ad, and window sign in the world... The amount of money companies are now spending on digital advertisements—like emails, Facebook ads, and Google search result advertisements—is much greater than all of these traditional forms of advertisements combined. And, digital spend is growing. Forbes reported that digital media advertising accounts for 64.4 percent of the global advertising spend. [90] Put simply, we need to dramatically update our understanding of what advertisements and propaganda are. Advertising and propaganda no longer mean the twentieth-century model of using television, radio, billboards, and leaflets. The new propaganda is digital. This is a massive, seismic paradigm shift that is being driven by companies, organizations, political parties, and governments who are trying to control our behavior and get us to think differently about our world.

And don't be fooled into thinking that you are immune to this new form of digital, weaponized information. While many people put up their defenses and say, "Sure, I see a lot of advertisements, but they don't affect my decisions," it seems that all this money going into digital advertising is showing a lot of results. And companies wouldn't be spending their budgets on digital advertisements if they weren't effective. My great hope is that at this point in the book, you are starting to realize why I have spent so much time talking about classical rhetoricians and thinkers like Plato and Aristotle, and the philosophers of technology like Heidegger and McLuhan. When 96 percent of our high school students can be so easily deceived and propagandized by a web site that's clearly marked, then we are failing our students, our children, our nation, and our world. Some of the core principles of rhetoric, like Aristotle's ethos, pathos, and logos, can help provide a critical framework for people to be able to more readily question the sources that they read and see. Humans are now bombarded with thousands of advertisements every day through multiple different media—websites, search results, pre-roll video advertisements on YouTube, etc.—and in the future, advertisements will come in augmented and virtual reality, video games, and places we cannot imagine yet—and the only way to prevent ourselves from being completely duped by these thousands of advertisements is to build up strong critical-thinking skills that involve rhetoric, philosophy, and digital and information literacy. We need our students and our children to be able to stop and say, "Wait, why should I believe this?" If we can't do this, then we are always just one step away from another Nazi-like party taking power, and a new Hitler easily persuading the masses. Or—and this seems just as likely to me—we could be one step away from something even worse.

I became personally aware of the dangers of these technologies when I worked as a Digital Marketing Specialist for a regional healthcare company. I managed websites for several hospitals and clinics. I also wrote and designed the "creative content" for digital and traditional advertisements and worked closely with the C-suite on the strategy for social media and the web. We were good at what we were doing, and our team even won an award for our digital breakthroughs from the parent company who owned, at the time, fifty-some hospitals in the United States. But there were a number of serious, ethical issues that I faced when I was doing this work, and it's why I didn't stay for more than a couple of years—just long enough to find a position as a professor and get out of that shady business.

The extent to which social media advertisements can be targeted to individuals is downright concerning. Almost anyone can create a Facebook advertising account, which gives you access to a whole suite of tools where you can target individuals with advertisements based on their age, income, educational level, spending habits, geographic location, interests, behaviors, marital status, and so much more. You can see how this could be useful for small businesses or even, say, musical artists. Imagine you are a small-town singer-songwriter, and you are trying to market your new album to people who might be interested. Let's say you're a folk artist and your music sounds something like the soft-spoken Americana of Iron & Wine mixed with some of the sad balladeering of Lana del Ray. You could create a video advertisement with one of your music videos and target people whose behavior on Facebook has demonstrated that they are interested in Iron & Wine and Lana del Ray. But then you could get really creative with it, and target only people who are likely to buy albums, such as those with incomes over $125,000, so that you know they have some degree of disposable income. Or, if you have an upcoming show at a venue in another town, you could use geographic targeting to reach people who live in that area, are of a certain age, and show a predisposition to buying concert tickets. There are, honestly, a lot of interesting strategies that a person can enact using social media advertising tools, and it's no wonder that companies spend tons of money on these very finely detailed, highly creative approaches to selling their products and spreading their ideologies.

All of this sounds just fine and dandy when we're thinking about small business owners who can use these technologies to reach out to new customers affordably. The example I give in my Digital Writing class when we start talking about Facebook advertising is the case of an artisanal cupcake shop. I ask students to imagine the demographic profiles of individuals who might be interested in buying high-end cupcakes (like couples planning a wedding or business-to-business/B2B marketing to other businesses who might buy larger quantities for their own shops or stores). But inevitably, I begin to share some of the stories of my own time working in digital marketing for healthcare, and the realities of these technologies become apparent. Though I don't have direct data about the quantity of unethical advertising content on social media, I would venture to guess that most of it is not small businesses, but rather, mega-corporations. And we all know the big companies seldom have our best interests at heart. So, in theory, the use of highly targeted social media marketing, if it were regulated perfectly and carefully used by vetted and ethical small and medium businesses, could be of some value to a capitalist society like ours. Of course, all the greedy, horrible people have taken these tools and technologies and used them to their advantage. As I say when talking about my cats, "This is why we can't have nice things."

One fringe case I like to talk about with my college students is when I was asked to create a new advertisement to promote our vasectomy procedures at our main hospital. A vasectomy is a sterilizing procedure for men so they can no longer have children. It's a useful procedure for men who have decided they do not want to have additional children, or who do not want children at all. We received some new data from our parent company (corporate overlords). The data demonstrated that men prefer to have this procedure completed during March Madness, so that they could take a few days off work, put ice on their downstairs bits, and watch some basketball. We had a few nervous laughs about this in the weekly marketing meeting. Sure, it's interesting when data and common sense just line up in this obvious sort of way. So, we were tasked with creating a campaign which included Facebook advertisements that could take advantage of this data.

Designing an effective Facebook advertisement is a rhetorical feat in itself. You must consider your audience and their values, goals, and aspirations. You must think very carefully about the timing of it. For the ancient Greeks, Kairos, or the opportune time, was an important rhetorical concept. Kairos is not the chronological timing of a speech (though that's important, too) but rather, the delivery in the greater social and historical context. Martin Luther King Jr. could not have delivered his "I Have a Dream" speech to a gathering in present-day Kentucky in 1543. It wouldn't have been the right time and place for those words to have any kind of effect.

Beyond time, you have to think about the visual rhetoric of an advertisement. You need to choose a photograph or image that will grab their attention away from the thousands of other advertisements that they are going to see that day, one that will have a suggestive influence over the viewer. It must arrest their attention. And you must target the advertisement to people who would actually consider the procedure, purchase, or candidate in the first place. You have to drill down into the specific age, educational background, and behaviors of those individuals.

One can actually get so caught up in the strategic-thinking process, creative-design process, and writing process, that it's possible to completely forget to ask the crucial question: "Should we even be doing this in the first place?"

When I had finished sketching out my demographic profile, I realized that *people I knew and loved* would be in this data set: men between the ages of thirty and fifty-five who already have at least one child, have employee-sponsored health insurance that would cover an elective procedure, and who liked basketball. These were friends and relatives of mine that would be seeing this advertisement. And what if they were so persuaded by this advertisement that they then went and actually had the procedure? What if that advertisement convinced *them,* persuaded *them* that it was a good idea? I could be inadvertently preventing the birth of a president or destroying a marriage. One can put too much thought into preposterous hypotheticals, but then again, these advertisements could have an actual impact on history, lives, the real living matter of reality in my community. It gave me a bit of a shiver, and we ended up having some conversations in the department about whether running these advertisements was a good idea. If I remember right, I had to spin it something like, "I'm not sure this would reflect well on the hospital's brand," which was a way of trying to steer us from the project by using language that would resonate with the for-profit healthcare's ethos.

This is just one small example of how advertisements can shape reality on a local level. This was all occurring at a small, regional healthcare system in Michigan with a marketing team of about five people. Now, imagine the sort of complex advertising that occurs in multi-million and billion-dollar corporations with hundreds of strategists and specialists and all the data *they* can find. It's almost unfathomable what can be done with these persuasive tools and technologies. In the aforementioned high-profile case of Cambridge Analytica, advertisers mixed these digital marketing demographic techniques with psychographic profiling—which is essentially weapons-grade information warfare—mixed with targeted social media advertising to influence elections in several countries around the world, including the United States, before they were shut down in 2018. It wasn't even the digital marketing that led to their demise—it was the fact that Cambridge Analytica was using private data of up to eighty-seven million Facebook users in their strategy, data they had obtained illegally through a process called data scraping. It leaves a question for us: why aren't these techniques of digital targeting being regulated? We can clearly say, just from this singular example, that military-grade disinformation campaigns are being enacted through social media channels in the United States and throughout the world, and they are having a very real impact on our elections. If this is not a threat to democracy, then I don't know what is.

## ARISTOTLE IN THE DIGITAL AGE

Not all persuasion that occurs on social media and the Internet is highly complex, black-boxed technology that must necessarily elude us. The systems of rhetoric devised by ancient thinkers are useful, too, in decoding and analyzing the "creative" elements of marketing and propaganda that we see on a daily basis.

A particularly disturbing trend is the phenomenon of "greenwashing," in which companies present themselves as being sustainable, environmentally friendly, or ecologically conscious when their practices are anything but. In one emotionally stirring advertisement from fast-food burrito-chain Chipotle, an acoustic cover of indie-pop band Coldplay's "The Scientist" performed by Willie Nelson sings out over a heartwarming, highly stylized animation of a farmer on their farmland. The animation turns dark as a depiction of the sinister machinery of factory farms is shown, aligning with lyrics about "questions of science" which do not "beat as loud as my heart" in a kind of rhetorical parallelism. Finally, in the rousing chorus, Nelson sings "I'm going back to the start," just as the farmer abandons the brutality of the factory farm to go back to the green pastures of splendid, pastoral farmland. For a burrito commercial, I find this advertisement to be a work of surprising commercial genius and rhetorical power that is unmatched by the advertising of any other fast-food Mexican restaurant. Unfortunately, of course, the actual business practices of Chipotle do not at all align with what is being portrayed in this powerfully constructed and persuasive advertisement. I suggest, for the purpose of practicing your rhetorical analysis, that you go to YouTube or your search engine of choice and find this 2011 advertisement using search terms like "Chipotle + Back to the Start + Willie Nelson + Advertisement" and so on. You'll see it. But then ask yourself, "what is the advertiser trying to persuade me of? What is the purpose of this messaging? What are they trying to get me to think or to do? How does that message line up with reality?"

It's not a very difficult exercise. It's clear that Chipotle wants us to believe that all the meat used in their products comes from idyllic farmland, and that the company doesn't participate in the machinations of the industrial food complex. We are told to believe that when we buy a beef, chicken, or pork burrito at Chipotle, the animal lived a good, happy life full of green pastures, sunshine, and socialization with their fellow animals. The advertisement goes even further, giving the viewer the suggestion that we shouldn't choose to dine at other fast-food restaurants, because those restaurants are damaging the environment and hurting animals. Chipotle must be the only reasonable choice for our dinner! It's a convincing argument that gives us a sense of moral satisfaction for making a choice that is not only ethical for animals but good for the environment.

Yet, a report by Deena Shanker and Juan Gastelum suggests that Chipotle, "is not as removed from industrial agriculture as the ads imply" and that "several of the messages these commercials convey are just not true, including that competitors use GMO animals (they do not), that Chipotle uses no GMOs (they do), and that their naturally and responsibly raised animals live in outdoor, open pastures. (That may be true, but can't be verified without the full definition of its standards.)"[91]

In an interview with Chipotle leadership, reporters were unable to receive clarification from the company about its standards, with a spokesperson saying only that animals were "humanely raised." That sounds nice, but it is, frankly, a meaningless term that does not tell us anything about the conditions the animals are subjected to. This is not a problem isolated to fast-food burrito restaurants. Countless companies use subtle marketing and packaging techniques to attempt to persuade us that their products are good for the environment, whether it's the use of light-green colors or words like *green, eco-friendly,* and *sustainable.* When you go to buy eggs and see the words "free range" on the carton, you are made to believe that those chickens could wander about freely on a farm, soaking up the sun and living the good life, but the words "free range" are hardly regulated at all. In many cases, they amount to little more than a

small, wire fence at the end of a dark, disease-ridden industri-
al-scale enclosure.

What does Aristotle and rhetoric have to do with eggs and
burritos? Well, absolutely everything. These types of disinformation and persuasion tactics jeopardize the integrity of democracy
and a free world. These companies are using artistic proofs to
attempt to persuade us to buy their products based on disinformation. This, in turn, leads us to believe that we have products
available to us that are not harmful to animals or the environment. In turn, we see less of a political exigency to address the
problems of factory farming, workers' rights, or ecological catastrophe, because we are made to believe—through these forms
of disinformation—that we are already doing our part, and that
there is nothing to worry about. Communication, marketing,
politics, democracy, media, and markets are all inextricably en-
meshed with one another. Why would someone vote for a Green
Party candidate or a state senator who supports the Green New
Deal, after all, if they go to the supermarket and see before them
what seems to be a plethora of sustainable, environmentally
friendly options? To the average consumer, it seems the work of
environmentalism is already done, that we can pat ourselves on
the back, and be done with that debate. This is the absolute danger of disinformation. Without true and accurate information
about the world we live in, we cannot make informed decisions
about what to do, where to focus our energies, who to elect to
positions of power, or even what values should be closest to our
hearts. Disinformation, in this way, deludes and corrupts both
democracies and free markets. And our best hope is a skeptical,
rhetorical, analytical response to these types of disinformation
and persuasion tactics. We should approach even the most mundane of daily objects—like a burrito or a carton of eggs—with

absolute scrutiny and skepticism. Those in power are always trying to sell us something, whether it's a product, an idea, or an
ideology.

Persuasive communication takes many forms and works on
us in ways that are not always immediate or easily perceptible.
The philosopher Slavoj Zizek notes in his film *The Pervert's
Guide to Ideology* that Beethoven's Ninth Symphony (and its
famous fourth and final movement, often referred to as the "Ode
to Joy," with lyrics adapted from Schiller's poem of that name),
has been used to unite people under extraordinarily diverse causes, including use by the early Nazi party of the 1930s, Russian
Soviet communists, and the extreme right-wing Apartheid movement in South Rhodesia, all of whom found anthemic purposes
for the song. Now, it is becoming the unofficial anthem of the
European Union. Music can have direct and immediate physio-
logical and emotional effects on our behavior. Several studies
demonstrate how music is used to influence consumer behavior
in retail stores, including grocery stores. In a very direct and obvious way, music *moves* us, even physically. We are persuaded to
dance or tap our fingers or feet in time to a beat. Music is used
throughout films, advertisements, social media videos, video
games, and at political rallies to cause emotional reactions which
lead to conditions under which persuasion is possible. In my early days of teaching at Michigan Technological University, I would
conduct an experiment with students where we used a simple
video-editing program to alter the audio of various commercials
and advertisements. We would, for example, take a video advertisement for a Ford F-150 and remove the audio bed. Without
the gaudy, bold, rock-and-roll music bed, students immediately
noticed that the advertisement seemed empty, pointless, and
stupid (which is actually the reaction we should have to most

advertisements). When the music bed is placed back into the advertisement, suddenly the giant truck seems cool, fast, energizing, masculine, and powerful. Without the music, it's just a stupid truck driving on a boring road—a mundane piece of machinery.

We would of course take this experiment further by then substituting the original music bed with various other genres of music. A pop-country track gives the advertisement a different tone, making the F-150 seem family friendly and giving students indications of BBQs, picnics, and going fishing (though no such imagery was present). When we drop in some contemporary death metal, the truck seems dangerous, ominous, and even frightening as it thunders down the mountain like an engine built in some forsaken, nightmarish underworld. When we place a classical music bed into the advertisement and let it play, the truck now seems intelligent, elegant, fancy, and sophisticated. In these simple ways, music can influence our perception of reality, or products, of political candidates, and of the very content of reality. It's difficult to say precisely that using music in this way constitutes disinformation in a strict sense, but it is certainly a calculated form of persuasion, and music is often used to aid disinformation in its effect and potency.

All of this is to say that there are complex, interrelated elements at play when we break down propaganda, marketing, or any other kind of communication, especially in technological and digital settings. What might appear as a simple Facebook post is actually working us over in many different ways, from the presentation of inartistic proofs in the text of the post, like statistics and quantitative information (whether accurate or misleading); to the use of color, imagery, symbolism, or metaphor to evoke particular emotions and memories. Then there's the use of music to influence our behavior and perception. Even video alone can be convincing without audio, as the Stanford History Education Group study demonstrated when researchers showed video footage of ballot tampering in Russia and roughly 75 percent of high school students who saw the video considered it to be compelling evidence of election fraud in the United States. The threshold by which we are persuaded is weak. In a specialized and distributed society, we must place our trust in others. Yet, all too often, that trust is poorly placed.

## BOGOST IN THE MACHINE

Rhetorical theorist Ian Bogost, in his book *Persuasive Games: The Expressive Power of Videogames*, offers us a new kind of rhetorical theory for dealing with digital media and complex digital information. Bogost defines procedural rhetoric as "the art of persuasion through rule-based representations and interactions, rather than the spoken word, writing, images, or moving pictures" and "the art of using processes persuasively."[92] This is pretty abstract, but very useful, so stick around for a minute while I explain. You don't have to play video games for procedural rhetoric to be important.

Let's consider a country where women aren't allowed to acquire a driver's license. This is a rule, or a procedure, codified into law. If you are a woman, you cannot drive; you cannot legally obtain a driver's license. In turn, there are all sorts of cascading effects; perhaps women do not have the same access to healthcare, affordable groceries, education, or job opportunities because of limited transportation options. The procedure itself makes an argument, namely that, "Women should not drive because women are not as valuable as men." or "Women are not as intelligent as men." There is a painful, prejudiced logic behind the codification of the procedure. This is a reality in some places in our world.

Now, we can consider more subtle examples. Bogostian procedural rhetoric helps us analyze complex digital media in many forms. We can analyze things like video games—a classic example is to imagine a character-creation screen that does not contain a wide variety of skin colors to choose from. The game is making an argument about what is normative by choosing not to include a diverse range of skin tones for the player to customize their character with.

In social media, almost all our activity is, in some way, affected by algorithms we do not see and do not understand. They are proprietary. They are used to boost certain content, fill our feed with certain content, and influence our behavior. Now, it's not like some person is sitting at Twitter or Facebook headquarters specifically selecting content for each person's feed, right? That would be impossible. So, programmers create sets of rules—procedures—which determine how content should fill your feed and what happens to it. This can influence everything from which videos go viral on YouTube to suppressing certain types of content on TikTok.

By being aware of algorithms and procedures, we can start to ask important questions about how information is reaching us. We must understand that when we use applications like Facebook, Instagram, TikTok, Twitter, or any other social-media platform, we are up against something that we don't fully understand—a kind of technological black box. We'll never know specifically how they are programmed. But we can be aware of procedural rhetoric to help us from being mystified by the type of content that appears on our screens.

Have you ever been served an eerily "accurate" advertisement on social media? Perhaps you were just thinking about buying a new pair of boots, and lo and behold, there is an advertisement for winter boots on Instagram! The data that advertisers have access to is truly astonishing. Using this data, they might be able to predict that you are just the kind of person who would be shopping for a pair of new boots at this time of year—you fit their customer profile, their target demographic; you belong to a "lookalike audience." Maybe you're a female between the age of thirty to thirty-five who has attended at least five outdoor winter festivals in the greater Minneapolis area in the last two years, has completed some college education, and has an income between $60,000-75,000. You're just the sort of person who might be looking for boots, and it's all there, in the data.

Bogost helps us to peel back a layer of this and to realize that rules and procedures are always working behind the scenes to serve content to us. It's not some magical, mystical miracle when we receive advertisements, disinformation, or propaganda that appeals to us. It was done by design. So, you must be smarter than them. You have to look at these digital advertisements and realize that you have been targeted by a set of complex algorithms that you may not totally understand, and so you should walk away long enough to pick them apart and analyze them. They will play on your weaknesses, fears, and desires. They want your money, your votes, and your time (and they want your children to get hooked onto their products, too, but that's a topic for a whole separate book).

Now, digital advertising is advancing rapidly. It would not surprise me if some companies are currently using rapid speech-to-text conversion paired with keyword analysis to service digital advertisements. Many applications allow microphone access on smartphones by default. Instagram and Facebook are examples of this. It's not too strange to imagine that your mobile device would pick up the audio of your conversation, convert it automatically to text, comb through the text for keywords, then service you advertisements on various platforms that Facebook and Instagram share data with or sell their data to, based on the keywords from your conversations. I want to be clear that I don't have any evidence that it's happening, but all the technology exists for it, and sometimes the advertisements do seem... well, we'll say they sometimes seem incredibly specific and oddly omniscient. Though of course, sometimes, they don't hit the mark at all.

Some users like to fight back against these advertising practices by opting out wherever they can, thereby taking control of their digital privacy. I like to occasionally search for esoteric and improbable subjects that I'm not particularly interested in, just to "mess" with the data pool. And honestly, I wouldn't be upset if YouTube put a little bit more Schubert in my feed of videos, anyway. Have you heard a performance of "Heidenröslein?" That's good stuff.

# Procedural Rhetorical Analysis of a Digital Advertisement

| Element of Analysis | Prompts | Possible Solutions |
|---|---|---|
| What is the medium and platform? | Is it a news article shared by a friend on Facebook? Is it a thirty-second video on Instagram? What does it look like, and why was it constructed that way? Why was this medium chosen? For example, advertisers might decide to promote content on LinkedIn if they want to target a professional, college-educated audience, or run ads on TikTok to reach a younger demographic. | Review privacy guidelines on that platform. See if you can opt out of targeted advertising. Limit the personal information you share with that platform, or "sabotage" the data pool by adding incomplete or inaccurate information about yourself. (Facebook does not need to know your address, the city you grew up in, your income, where you went to school, etc. Consider limiting the amount of information you share on social media.) |
| How might you have been targeted? How did the advertisement or message find you? | Were you targeted by age, income, education, geographic area, gender, family, consumer behavior, interests, or something else? What aspects of your online activity and behavior brought you to this moment, where you are now seeing this advertisement or information? Does it seem to be fitted to you, or is it a mistake in some way? If you seem to have been targeted mistakenly with this information or advertisement, how did that happen? | We can't know precisely how we have been targeted, but if you're super curious, you can create an advertising account on Facebook and look at some of the tools to get a better understanding of how they work. Anyone can create an advertising account and target people based on their behaviors, interests, age, income, etc. As good rhetoricians in the digital age, we should stop and consider how we have been targeted based on this data. Targeting can be extremely fine-tuned. For example, you might be targeted for liking a musician's fan page or watching a single video on YouTube. |

| | | |
|---|---|---|
| What was the purpose of the targeting? | Why did an organization, company, or individual spend money to run this advertisement? Is it to promote a product? Is it to attract attention to their political campaign? Is it to distract from something else? Is it a public relations piece, designed to shift the public narrative about an event? | Again, we don't know exactly unless we're sitting in the marketing strategy meeting where this was discussed, but we can usually get a clear idea of what's going on when we pay attention. Perhaps it's a sponsored post by a news agency that's known to have an ideological bias, or perhaps it's an advertisement for a film. We know what they want us to do—to vote for a particular candidate or to buy a movie ticket or subscribe to a streaming service. Figure out the original "purpose" of the advertisement based on your analysis. |
| What is it specifically asking you to do? | Is there a "Call to Action" specifically asking you to do something? Is there a button that you're being asked to click? Or is it something less explicit; is it asking you to feel a certain way, or think a certain way, or desire something? What is the underlying "logic" of the content? | This is usually written in the command tense, such as "Buy now!" or "Click here to learn more!" or "Sign up for our newsletter!' But persuasion can be much more subtle than this. Is it asking you to do, think, vote, or behave a certain way? We'd like to think we're rational people, but you'd be surprised how often people click on something just because it's written in the command tense and there's a colored button. We are very "persuadable," after all. |

ISN'T THE RHETORICAL ART, TAKEN AS A WHOLE,
A WAY OF DIRECTING THE SOUL BY MEANS OF
SPEECH...?

—PLATO [93]

## CHAPTER IX

# Return to Rhetoric:
# Solutions to the Problems
# of Disinformation

*The most characteristic concern of rhetoric [is] the*
*manipulation of men's beliefs for political ends.... the basic*
*function of rhetoric [is] the use of words by human agents to*
*other human agents.*
—KENNETH BURKE[94]

Part of the reason that the ancient Greek thinkers are still so relevant today is that they identified timeless, universal problems for which we still have no perfect solution. There are no perfect formulas to solve questions like "What's the best way to structure a society?" or "How do we live a good life?" You can't expect to Google, "What's the meaning of life?" and be very satisfied with the answers. Science and high-quality, peer-reviewed, expert research can guide us along the way, but there's no quantifiable, complete solution to a question like that. And more than that, these are questions that we wouldn't want to subject to a rigid model or outsource to the machinations of a formula. Whenever we run into places where there is no quantifiable answer for a problem, rhetoric and philosophy emerge. Imagine, for a moment, that we could consult with an all-powerful artificial intelligence. Offloading these essential, human questions to a non-human could be disastrous. Perhaps our all-powerful artificial intelligence would determine that the best outcome for human beings would be to put them all to sleep and let them rest in a drugged state of hallucination for eternity. Probably not the best outcome for the human species. Or perhaps our AI would conclude that the total amount of suffering on the planet is too high, so it would begin testing out the ideal human population on earth by immediately killing half of the people in the world at random. Human problems require the nuanced thought of humans and all our tools and disciplines of philosophy, science, reasoning, and rhetoric. Human solutions for human problems.

Unfortunately, it's all the pitfalls of being human that then burden us with these nearly unsolvable problems. We look on in frustration as most climate scientists warn us of human-made climate change while our elected leaders look the other way. We see all our human vices on display in our wars; corporate greed; wealth inequality; and our inability to provide stable housing, education, healthcare, and opportunities to citizens. Noam Chomsky writes in *Media Control: The Spectacular Achievements of Propaganda*, "The role of the media in contemporary politics forces us to ask what kind of a world and what kind of a society we want to live in, and in particular in what sense of democracy do we want this to be a democratic society?"[95] The ancient Greeks did not figure everything out—far from it. Their economy relied heavily on slave labor and only land-owning males could participate in the democratic process. This was not a democracy in a contemporary sense. But this does not mean we should dismiss the work of great thinkers like Plato and Aristotle and pull them out of the canon and classroom. Now, more than ever, we need a lot more Plato and Aristotle in our lives. We need the field of rhetoric. We need philosophy to be part of everyday discourse. We must become rhetorical thinkers if we want to combat the disinformation epidemic. We must take it upon ourselves to be analysts of communication and to evaluate the credibility of arguments and of media. It's up to us—each of us—to face the world with a critical, rhetorical lens so that we are not misled by the machinations of the big propaganda machines.

Do we truly live in democracy today? Where on earth do we find a nation state where every person is a well-informed, educated voter who has equal access to participate in the electoral process and is equally represented in decision-making? Nowhere do we find a democracy that has not been corrupted in some essential way. Chomsky goes on to describe two models or conceptions of democracy: "One conception of democracy has it that a democratic society is one in which the public has the means to participate in some meaningful way in the management of their own affairs and the means of information are open and free. If you look up democracy in the dictionary, you'll get a definition something like that." This is the democracy that we all imagine and all desire. This is the democracy where we would be able to choose our own fate and decide what is best for us. Americans know Abraham Lincoln's famous phrase from his Gettsyburg Address describing a "government of the people, by the people, for the people," and that it is our duty to dedicate ourselves to the "unfinished work" in making sure this does not disappear from the earth. While Lincoln wrote this in context of the American Civil War, it is now apparent to citizens the world over that democracy is in danger of disappearing. Chomsky goes on to write, "An alternative conception of democracy is that the public must be barred from managing of their own affairs and the means of information must be kept narrowly and rigidly controlled. That may sound like an odd conception of democracy, but it's important to understand that it is the prevailing conception. In fact, it has long been, not just in operation, but even in theory." [96] This second conception of democracy is the democracy that we live with, and the democracy in which propaganda, disinformation, and media control are the norm rather than the exception.

We can easily recognize propaganda in other countries, and it bothers us and shakes us to the core. When we look at a country like North Korea under the dictatorship and strict control of Kim Jong-un, it is easy to see that the state-owned media and education systems are primarily systems of control and disinformation. Like Plato's *daemon* shook him awake in *Phaedrus*, our conscience is bothered when we see people who are not free: free to think, vote, and act. Everywhere in North Korea, these systems of media and power are used to instill the narrative that the ruling regime is to be honored, and that Kim Jong-un, or whoever is in power at the given moment, is to be revered as a god, a deity, a supreme being. These tactics should be very familiar to you, now, as a reader of this book, for you have read that the deification of rulers dates back nearly five thousand years to the ancient Sumerians and King Sargon I. And still, today, we are falling for these ruses. Kim Jong-un is no more divine than either of my cats. Given more time, I'd probably argue the case that cats are demonstrably more divine than any supreme leader of North Korea, but that's not important at the moment. What is important is to recognize the ease with which we see the workings of disinformation in other places, and the difficulty with which we recognize it at home.

But how different is our media landscape in the Western Hemisphere? American media is not, at present, state-owned, like it is in North Korea or Russia, but it is privately held by billionaires who have particular interests, perspectives, political motives, and agendas. The televised news shows which millions of Americans watch every day, like CNN, Fox News, and MSNBC, are profit-driven companies that also operate as disinformation and propaganda machines to control narratives. Every one of our massive corporations and every member of the billionaire class participates in digital advertising and social media manipulation to spread narratives that are meant to disinform. The media landscape is not, as Chomsky's first conception of democracy would have it, "open and free." Rather, our "means of information" are absolutely controlled, and we are being absolutely disinformed by the narratives, ideologies, and values of a ruling class, not just in our traditional cable news media, but via the digital landscape of social media advertising and manipulation, search engine results, and in the very coding of the algorithms of these technologies. It's time for us to wake up and see what can be done about it.

The premise of this book has been that there is something that can be done at the individual level about disinformation. By arming ourselves with knowledge of the past, of the history of rhetoric and disinformation, and by taking on a critical, rhetorical perspective toward media and technology, we can better arm ourselves against the influx of deceptive messaging, disinformation, misinformation, and advertising and propaganda that is bombarding us every day from every direction. That is one step in the right direction, and you have come a long way already just by picking up this book. But there is so much more to be done in terms of regulation, education, and spreading information and digital literacy to the disenfranchised. There is nothing those in power fear more than an articulate, well-read, and well-educated citizenry.

It's nearly impossible to imagine a world where there is not some form of disinformation, lying, exaggeration, truth doctoring, or information warfare. Governments, political parties, companies, organizations, and the people who run them, all have private interests, and they'd like to persuade you to join in their ideological camp.

But it's worth trying a thought experiment to imagine what the world would look like, if everyone was interested in the truth as the highest value. We can stretch our imagination a little bit like Plato did in his *Republic*, and picture for ourselves an ideal future. From the perspective of our present time, these ideals would look much different than what the ancient Greeks had dreamed up. For me, I think a utopia might look something like an open playing field for all, where there is ready access to comfortable housing, a reliable food supply, a robust education available at one's fingertips, good medical care, and access to reliable, vetted, quality information. I'm not a bit ashamed to argue that we have a *right* to the truth, though it's a rather idealistic position to take. The steps we would need to take to foster a society where the truth was of a higher value than profit is unclear to me. We can't police the truth—the sheer quantity of information and communication in the world is too vast. This is what the well-intentioned, but poorly thought-out,

Disinformation Governance Board in the United States has already gotten wrong in their recent suggestion to allow users to annotate each other's Tweets. It shows a fundamental misunderstanding of how disinformation operates and propagates. And, of course, Twitter isn't listening to some minor government board, anyway.

What would a world where truth was the highest value really look like? We could trust our politicians to follow through with campaign promises and party platforms. We could listen to the news and not doubt the veracity or intent of the content. We could organize more easily in pursuit of common goals and live in a more democratic world—put our trust in leaders who represent us, speak for us, and do what's right by us. Maybe these are big dreams—maybe they are too far beyond human reach. But by reading this book, you are participating in a process that gets us a little closer to these dreams—a little closer to imagining a world in which we value the truth.

## SAVING PERSUASION

The indisputable expert on propaganda, Philip Taylor, writes that "In pluralistic democracies which purport to exist on the basis of consensus rather than coercion, persuasion thus becomes an integral part of the political process."[97] Yet too often we see how language, communication, and information technologies are used in the service of those in power to control, suppress, and persuade those who might interfere with their designs: "In the struggle for power, propaganda is an instrument to be used by those who want to secure or retain power just as much as it is by those wanting to displace them. For the smoke to rise, there must first be a spark which lights the flame. Propaganda is that spark." [98]

In *Saving Persuasion,* Professor Bryan Garsten of Yale University writes, "the practice of persuasion seems prone to two forms of corruption. In trying to persuade, democratic politicians may end up manipulating their audiences, or may end up pandering to them. These twin dangers reveal something about the nature of persuasion as an activity" and that these "two vices thus arise from the dual character of persuasion itself, which consists partly in ruling and partly in following." [99] Garsten, here, is talking about human speech, and mentions seventeenth-century thinker Thomas Hobbes's view that democracies have a tendency to devolve into an "aristocracy of orators"—that is, those who can speak best rise to the top. Certainly, we have seen this at times—in the fascism and populism of the early twentieth century in Europe, for example. (Although philosopher Slavoj Zizek likes to remind us that some Italians remember Mussolini's reign as the period during which all the trains actually ran on time.)

Garsten continues by explaining how, across time, rhetoric was a vital part of a Western education:

"In ancient Athens and Rome, in medieval schools and Renaissance cities, in early modern Europe and nineteenth-century America, both scholars and statesmen taught their students that a well-functioning republican polity required citizens who could articulate arguments on either side of a controversy, link those arguments to the particular opinions and prejudices of their fellow citizens, and thereby facilitate the arguing and deliberating that constituted a healthy political life." [100]

We can here turn back to Socrates and Plato to understand some of the dangers of this perspective. While Garsten's
arguments are nuanced and I don't mean to disparage them,
there is a kind of naivety or narrowness to thinking of rhetoric as solely belonging to civic speech where fairly elected
political officials are having meaningful, honest debates about
issues that are important to citizens. This is an idealist's fancy
and is not at all representative of the world that we live in,
where lobbying and corporate interests have infiltrated every
inch of the democratic process and wedge issues are used to
distract and dismay populations while lawmakers play their
games in service of the corporate elite. Garsten forgets that
much of persuasion does not occur in live speech in the form
of earnest dialogues between citizens of a country, but in the
one-way channels of mass communication, social media, news
programs, and other forms of propagandistic persuasion
meant to disinform citizens and mold their behavior—and
that those forms of disinformation and propaganda are rhetoric, too.

Perhaps, now, we can return to *Phaedrus* for a final lesson
that will bring us full circle. Socrates, at the end of Plato's
*Phaedrus*, leads us on an interesting journey where he considers
the dangers of writing as a technology. He tells us that writing is
not dynamic—you cannot talk with it, you cannot have a dialogue with a text in the same way that you can have a dialogue
with a living person. Thus, you cannot necessarily uncover the
deeper layers of meaning that are always lurking there, the intentions, the belief systems, the ideas that underlie all that is being
said. Socrates invents a myth in this dialogue to explain how
writing was invented:

Socrates: At the Egyptian city of Naucratis, there was a famous old god, whose name was Theuth; the bird which is called the Ibis is sacred to him, and he was the inventor of many arts, such as arithmetic and calculation and geometry and astronomy and draughts and dice, but his great discovery was the use of letters. Now in those days the god Thamus was the king of the whole country of Egypt; and he dwelt in that great city of Upper Egypt which the Hellenes call Egyptian Thebes, and the god himself is called by them Ammon. To him came Theuth and showed his inventions, desiring that the other Egyptians might be allowed to have the benefit of them; he enumerated them, and Thamus enquired about their several uses, and praised some of them and censured others, as he approved or disapproved of them. It would take a long time to repeat all that Thamus said to Theuth in praise or blame of the various arts. But when they came to letters, This, said Theuth, will make the Egyptians wiser and give them better memories; it is a specific both for the memory and for the wit. Thamus replied: O most ingenious Theuth, the parent or inventor of an art is not always the best judge of the utility or inutility of his own inventions to the users of them. And in this instance, you who are the father of letters, from a paternal love of your own children have been led to attribute to them a quality which they cannot have; for this discovery of yours will create forgetfulness in the learners' souls, because they will not use their memories; they will trust to the external written characters and not remember of themselves. The specific which you have discovered is an aid not to memory, but to reminiscence, and you give your disciples not truth, but only the semblance of truth; they will be hearers of many things and will have learned nothing; they will appear to be omniscient and will generally know nothing; they will be tiresome company, having the show of wisdom without the reality."[101]

Socrates goes on to compare writing to "painting" that observes a "solemn silence." We cannot ask questions of a painting to learn how it was created, or with what energies or moods or moments or inspirations. The painting cannot speak to us in a living state—it is a constraint of the medium. So, too, does writing seem to lock in its meaning and hold it still. Though, of course, there is an irony to this, as Plato and Socrates only live on with us thousands of years later because of this marvelous technology of writing. What Socrates says next is absolutely characteristic of our understanding of him—he favors the dialectic process, the discussion between living people, who can dig deeply into language to discover what is known and what is not known, to "define" the "several particulars of which he is writing or speaking."

Socrates: Until a man knows the truth of the several particulars of which he is writing or speaking, and is able to define them as they are, and having defined them again to divide them until they can be no longer divided, and until in like manner he is able to discern the nature of the soul, and discover the different modes of discourse which are adapted to different natures, and to arrange and dispose them in such a way that the simple form of speech may be addressed to the simpler nature, and the complex and composite to the more complex nature-until he has accomplished all this, he will be unable to handle arguments according to rules of art, as far as their nature allows them to be subjected to art, either for the purpose of teaching or persuading;-such is the view which is implied in the whole preceding argument.

There is practical wisdom in this, even, and I share that with my students. Do not go writing and speaking about something which you have not researched. And don't trust someone just because they're wearing a suit and speaking confidently about some subject—they probably know as little or less than you do about it. We often hear writers give the advice of something like "Write about that which you know," possibly popularized by Hemingway. But Socrates is after something else, here—he is not giving us creative writing advice. What Socrates is telling us is that writing and speaking about matters which we have not deeply considered, which we have not subjected to a kind of philosophical process of questioning, are mere Sophistry. This is precisely why Socrates was enraged by those who would go about Athens charging a fee for their teaching, providing a kind of prescriptive, technical rhetorical skill set to anyone, and showing others how they could make lesser causes seem the greater, how they could lie and fabricate and spin webs of deceit to persuade anyone of anything, even if it were not the truth.

Socrates's greatest wisdom, of course, is that in the end, we know nothing. After all of his countless conversations with politicians, wealthy business owners, the elite of Athens, the playwrights and poets, the artists and musicians, the young and the old, the sick and the healthy, the war heroes and the wanderers, he recognizes that no one really knows anything. Given enough time, he can show anyone who is willing to listen that the basis of their assumptions about reality are founded in error—that they have made grave mistakes in their reasoning, that they hold true to them beliefs that they have not assessed and have not analyzed. And such is the case with all of us—we go about our lives thinking we know what we mean when we say Justice, Evil, or Nature, but when we break apart our understanding of these concepts, we see there is little else but a mirage of understanding. We like to think we know what we're doing here, but we don't.

This is why credibility matters so much and why we need to assess it. We might say, "Sure, Socrates, no one really knows anything and we're all spinning around on a big rock in the universe and what is the universe, anyway, and why are we here? Excellent questions, but I have a real life that I care about." I get it. Credibility is that important idea—for the Greeks, they called it ethos—that helps us judge the expertise and trustworthiness of others based on their credentials, actions, and character. Credibility is why you wouldn't want your neighbor to perform your complex spinal surgery, and why you wouldn't want your surgeon to fix the muffler on your van. But credibility is a sneaky thing. We are too quick to trust anyone who merely looks like they know what they're talking about. We hardly think about it all. Well, now that you know what to look for, maybe you will start thinking rhetorically. Just because you read it on Facebook doesn't mean it's true; frankly, it's probably the opposite. Just because it fell out of some politician's mouth doesn't mean it's a fact. Most of them aren't true experts on anything.

Some final words from Gorgias might help us to think about these issues. Was Plato's Socrates excessively critical of the Sophists? Gorgias, after all, has left us much wisdom about the nature of persuasion. He was a Sophist, sure, but one who seemed self-aware of the powers of language, who compared speech to a drug that could have powerful effects over our minds and reasoning. Was Gorgias a malicious wielder of words, corrupting the citizenry and teaching them how to lie, or was something else going on? Gorgias was one of the rockstar rhetoricians of the ancient world. He traveled throughout the Mediterranean giving demonstration speeches—these were like the "stump speeches" of politicians, that were carefully crafted, dutifully memorized, and perfectly arranged to spellbind audiences, and also to attract new students. Gorgias made himself a wealthy man through his prowess and renown as a speaker, and his abilities as a rhetorician and teacher, but he also gained a reputation as being absolutely representative of the Sophists. These are the same Sophists who Plato and others rallied against.

But at the end of the Gorgias's extant *Encomium of Helen*, there is a telling line where Gorgias says that he may have been making this entire speech merely to entertain himself, as a kind of diversion. He could have just as easily argued the opposite case—to blame Helen, instead of attempting to remove the blame from her. This is the key to understanding the danger of language. A big company can spend millions of dollars creating any narrative which is profitable and beneficial for them, and they can use every form of media to send their message—from podcasts to cable news to highly targeted Instagram advertisements and bots. They can post on Reddit and Twitter and take strides to influence Google search result placements. Companies and political parties know how to use every available means of persuasion. And so, we need to be prepared to analyze every available means of persuasion.

# BRINGING RHETORIC BACK TO EDUCATION

And that's exactly what Plato was fighting when he explored the relationship between truth and rhetoric in his dialogues. Patrick Kenney, in his "Foreword" to the *Bloomsbury Library of Educational Thought* series book on Plato, succinctly distills what we all know about Plato. He, "invented the subject of philosophy, and all that we mean by that term can be found in his writings" (xiv). That "Plato set the entire western project in motion, and our world is what is in large part because of his legacy" is stated as a self-evident fact. But what should be clearer to us now, is that "our own time is singularly unreceptive to Plato, if not forthrightly anti-Platonic." Our education systems are geared toward providing technical and career training for students to participate in capitalism. I'm guilty of this myself—I teach a course that helps prepare our graduating seniors to enter the job market. They need jobs to survive, of course, and this is especially true for our student population in rural Wisconsin, which is composed of many non-traditional and first-generation college students. But more than that, the American landscape of civic discourse is devolved and uninspired. Our media landscape comprises repetitive and uninspired Hollywood movies; the musical landscape is rife with simplistic pop songs and Taylor Swifts; appallingly uninteresting and poorly planned public-education curriculum bores our kids to near-death. And we shouldn't be boring and torturing the future generations of humanity to near-death.

What would a more Platonic education look like, a more philosophical and rhetorical education? As Keeney writes, "Plato was the first to systematically set forth a theory of education, and to articulate the symbiotic relationship between politics and education." (xiv) What must become clear to us now is that the "central educational questions which exercised the ancient Greeks are questions which are similarly imperative for our own generation." We have wrongfully offloaded the burden of serious questions away from philosophy, and transformed philosophy into a buzzword-laden academic discipline, where today's philosophers become locked in the publish-or-perish hyper-productivity of competitive academia. When even philosophers don't have time to think, who is left contemplating the serious questions of how we organize our societies, what the goals of a society should be, what constitutes a good and meaningful life, and to what values or virtues should we be orienting ourselves?

The answer, here, is that philosophy, rhetoric, informational literacy, and critical thinking should not be walled off in the higher education institutions of a country. Philosophy and rhetoric—these most dangerous frameworks, tool kits, treasure chests—must be incorporated into public education from an early age, across all social and economic classes, and held in a much higher regard than at present. American public education, at present, is not much of an education at all. This is not a problem unique to the humanities. Students are memorizing a lot of information, but they aren't doing much with it—they aren't applying it, working with it, and making their lives or the broader world better because of their knowledge. And so, the information fails to become knowledge at all.

The Nobel Prize-winning physicist Richard Feynman describes this problem in his comical and quick-reading autobiography, *Surely You're Joking, Mr. Feynman!* Feynman spends time in Brazil working one summer as a Visiting Professor for the Center for Physical Research. He enjoys his time there so much that he returns for a ten-month stay to lecture at the University of Rio. Among other work, he taught a group of students who were in training to become teachers in Brazil. But, he discovered a "very strange phenomenon," that the students had "memorized" everything, but were unable to complete even simple problems assigned to them, as they were completely unable to apply the knowledge.[102] The students asked Feynman to give a talk at the end of the year to share his experiences teaching in Brazil. Feynman relates the story thus:

"Then I say, 'The main purpose of my talk is to demonstrate to you that *no* science is being taught in Brazil!'

I can see them stir, thinking, 'What? No science? This is absolutely crazy! We have all these classes.'

So I tell them that one of the first things to strike me when I came to Brazil was to see elementary kids in bookstores, buying physics books. There are so many kids learning physics in Brazil, beginning much earlier than kids do in the United States, that it's amazing you don't find many physicists in Brazil – why is that? So many kids are working so hard, and nothing comes of it.

Then I gave the analogy of a Greek scholar who loves the Greek language, who knows that in his country there aren't many children studying Greek. But he comes to another country, where he is delighted to find everybody studying Greek – even the smaller kids in the elementary schools. He goes to the examination of a student who is coming to get his degree in Greek, and asks him, 'What were Socrates's ideas on the relationship between Truth and Beauty?' – and the student can't answer. Then he asks the student, 'What did Socrates say to Plato in the Third

Symposium?' the student lights up and goes, 'Brrrrrrr-rr-up" – he tells you everything, word for word, that Socrates said, in beautiful Greek. But what Socrates was talking about in the Third Symposium was the relationship between Truth and Beauty!

What this Greek scholar discovers is, the students in another country learn Greek by first learning to pronounce the letters, then the words, and then the sentences and paragraphs. They can recite, word for word, what Socrates said, without realizing that those Greek words actually *mean* something. To the student they are all artificial sounds. Nobody has ever translated them into words the student can understand.

I said, 'That's how it looks to me, when I see you teaching the kids 'science' here in Brazil." [103]

I love this story, because it captures so much of what I observed in my public education experience in K-12 in the United States in the 1990s and 2000s. I ended up spending a lot of time in the Peter White Public Library, the local library in Marquette, MI where I grew up. It was the only place where I could really learn anything! From 7 a.m. when I was barely awake (I'm still a night owl to this day), to two or three in the afternoon, it was quizzes and tests and quizzes and tests on subjects that ranged from astronomy to the American Civil War. But the tests and quizzes don't foster a passion or an interest in these subjects. What could be more interesting and alarming than the fact we are all living on a small rock blasting through space, that our sun is just one star among hundreds of billions, that our galaxy is just one galaxy, that it takes light seventy years just to travel to the closest star to us? It's terrifying and awe-inspiring stuff.

But instead, students are quizzed on the names of constellations, which are just arbitrary arrangements of far-off stars seen from our vantage point. Constellations can be interesting if the history of their myths and legends are told with them, granting them a sense of story, purpose, and cultural and historical context, but there was no such content in our high school astronomy course.

To go back to Kenney's "Foreword" to the Bloomsbury Plato book, it is clear to me that today we are living in a world that has mostly forgotten the spirit of philosophy. We live in a world that has abandoned what we could call the Socratic spirit, and has done so much to our detriment. To help protect against disinformation and to give the next generation a fighting chance at orienting themselves toward worthy goals like science, truth, and reason, we need to help cultivate a more serious education. We might try fixing our public schools, but if we can't do that, then at least we can do it in our homes and in our communities, in the books we put on the shelves, in the media we consume, and even in our daily conversations—by asking good questions, stopping to think about problems, and having the patience to allow long lines of questioning and discovery. Too often, when a child or a teenager asks an important question, like "Why is this such a way?" or "Why must this be so?" we just shrug it off and don't pursue that very sincere inquiry. Even worse, we often shut them down and tell them to do as they're told. Well, let's allow a little more questioning in our lives. We need it now more than ever.

The profound mysteries and pleasures of philosophy and rhetoric do not need to be walled off in universities or made inaccessible by obscure terminology and uninteresting academic language. Philosophy and rhetoric is the birthright of every human on this planet: the power to question authority, the spirit to inquire about why we are here and where we came from, the very right to turn ideas upside down and around and to look at them from different viewpoints. This is the wild and natural human philosophy which we all have a right to practice.

## DON'T BE AFRAID OF PLATO

I teach many other courses besides those that deal with ancient Greek rhetoric. One of my favorite courses to teach every spring is Technical Writing. I conduct a module—that is, a few weeks of focused study on a particular topic—on Adobe desktop publishing software, like InDesign. I appreciate the perspective offered in the now-classic 2007 documentary film on graphic design and typography, *Helvetica,* where several interviewees explain how digital design technologies are democratizing the industry. This is even more true, today, over fifteen years after the film was produced. My students can access the same Adobe software that is used by Fortune 500 companies and industry experts. But the technology doesn't make the designer. It can speed up the process, but knowing how to use the software isn't the same as being a good designer.

In this class, I call my module about InDesign the "Don't Be Afraid of Adobe" segment. I find that this approach works very well for those who have never touched this kind of software before. And to be sure, it can be complicated at first. There is unknown terminology, complicated menus, hotkeys, shortcuts, and all the fundamental principles of graphic design and typography that go into the actual creation of a simple document. How can someone who can't tell a *sans serif* font from a *serif* font learn how to design a newsletter in just a couple of weeks? Well, I'll tell you, every single one of my students figures it out. And I think you can, too.

But of course, I'm not just talking about desktop publishing and graphic design right now. I think the same principles apply to learning the ancient art forms of rhetoric, philosophy, or any other discipline. When we are born into this world, we have no knowledge of alphabets, syntax, and grammar. But we absorb all of this as we communicate with others. We naturally learn our languages, but we must be taught how to write, spell, and type on a computer. When we first start to read Gorgias, Plato, or Aristotle, the proper nouns scare my students, and they worry that they will be tested on the dates of the Peloponnesian War or have to remember every single Roman emperor. I'll let you in on a little secret: I'm a published author, peer-reviewed scholar, and a professor, and I don't remember every Roman emperor who ruled that long ago. I've never thought that rote memorization was the key to a good education, and I still don't. I don't test my students on their ability to memorize. But I do test them on their comprehension of key ideas, and my exam questions can be quite difficult.

At the end of my Introduction to Rhetoric course, I ask my students to respond to the following prompt: "What is the relationship between rhetoric and truth?" Without fail, almost every single one of them crafts a detailed response in MLA style, citing Plato and Aristotle and other great ancient thinkers, all of whom they had never heard of prior to enrolling in my class. You know, honestly, I'm very proud of them. Most of them even use the Stephanus numbers or Bekker pagination properly, and they sound a little bit like solid scholars as they're working through the problem. Only once did I have a student submit a clearly

Googled response, and it was obvious, because it didn't have much to do with the question.

So, what do we do in the fifteen or sixteen weeks of this course? Well, mostly, we read. We read a selection from George Kennedy's *A New History of Classical Rhetoric*. Then we read primary texts like Gorgias's speech, "The Encomium of Helen," and we read dialogues by Plato like *Protagoras* and *Phaedrus*. We read Aristotle's *Rhetoric* and we read Cicero's *De Inventione*. And, you know what? You can read these texts, too. In fact, you can read them for free from amazing websites like the MIT Classics Archive, or Project Gutenberg. Throughout a big part of human history, books were treasured, material objects that could cost as much as a month's wages or more. Today, almost all of us have the resources and abilities to access these primary texts, and the literacy to be able to read them. So why aren't we doing it? What's stopping you from finishing this book and reading some Gorgias or Plato? I bet it would only take you twenty minutes or so to read "The Encomium of Helen" and then take some notes or go for a walk and think about it.

Here's the thing: if our public education system will continue to be dismantled, then we'll need to take up the torch ourselves. Read a Platonic dialogue aloud in the living room with your kids, or start a reading group in your neighborhood. Go down to the pub with a copy of *Phaedrus* and read through it with some friends. Then talk about it. The only way we're going to start caring about the truth again is if we start talking about it.

Plato had an ambiguous relationship with rhetoric, after all. He saw how passionate language and inflamed speech could lead to disaster. His mentor, Socrates, was put on trial in Athens and sentenced to death in 399 BCE. The famous trial plays out in

Plato's dialogue, the *Apology*. Freethinkers and those who go against the grain have always been viewed as dangerous by those in power. Socrates surprises us all, though, when he calmly accepts the judgment made against him. Then, however, he issues a kind of warning to the assembly:

> "Still I have a favor to ask of them. When my sons are grown up, I would ask you, O my friends, to punish them; and I would have you trouble them, as I have troubled you, if they seem to care about riches, or anything, more than about virtue; or if they pretend to be something when they are really nothing, then reprove them, as I have reproved you, for not caring about that for which they ought to care, and thinking that they are something when they are really nothing. And if you do this, I and my sons will have received justice at your hands." [104]

Even when staring down death, Socrates is thinking about future generations, about the education and well-being of his children, of all Athenians and peoples. And death is something that Socrates says he does not fear, for it is either an eternity of nothingness that passes like a single night of sleep, or it is transportation of the soul to somewhere new, and nothing could be better. This—one of Socrates's final messages to us—is a call to ethics, a call to the good. We should think about how we help our sons and daughters, and their sons and daughters, become better people who also value the truth. Now, more than ever, should we heed this call of Socrates, to lay a path forward for future generations.

## TOWARD A MORE HONEST FUTURE

As I promised at the outset of the book, I don't have all the answers. I can't tell you what is true and what is not true, or what you should value or what you should believe. But what I have tried to do is give you a broad historical perspective on disinformation and truth, to show you that these are not new problems, and that there *are* answers. When it feels like the world is falling apart and that we live in a "post-truth" world, just remember that many other people have felt the same way, and much the same has been true across thousands of years, going all the way back to our first empire, and stretching even further through time. Disinformation and massive lies from the ruling class is the norm, not the exception. What I also tried to do in this work was to share some wisdom about these problems from thinkers like Gorgias, Plato, Aristotle, Cicero, and Quintilian, and to provide some models for rhetorical analysis, so that you can assess and evaluate the credibility of the messages that you come across in your own life. Whether you're listening to a political speech, see a video advertisement on social media, read a suspicious headline on a website, or are having a conversation with friends or family, the bits of wisdom and practical frameworks I've shared with you in this book should help you take on the responsibility to ask the right questions to make sure you're not being taken for a ride. Rhetorical analysis is a powerful tool. Don't be afraid to use it.

Our governments aren't doing anything to slow down technologically aided disinformation, and artificial intelligence and big tech companies are just getting smarter, faster, stronger, and more powerful. If those in power are going to continue to disinform and lie to us—and they always will—then we need to arm ourselves and protect ourselves from the lies and disinformation so that we can live rich, intellectual lives where we think for ourselves, come to our own truths and our own decisions, and craft the world that *we* want, not the world that *they* want. Rhetoric can be much more than a toolkit; it is a mode of thought, and a way of life. Become a keen rhetorical thinker, and you will no longer be just another persuadable, gullible citizen. You'll be armed to the teeth with foolproof methods for analyzing and picking apart messages. Practice it daily. When you see an advertisement in your social media feed, ask yourself: why was I targeted with this? What is the purpose of it? What is it trying to make me do, think, believe, or buy? How is it trying to achieve that goal? How is it using ethos, pathos, and logos? Am I really going to fall for this faulty logic? And soon, the answer will be *no*; you will not fall for this faulty logic. You won't let your emotions be played with by all these advertisements and propaganda. You will become more objective, keener, and more analytical. You'll be freer thinking with each passing day. But you must be diligent and practice if you are to cultivate a rhetorical way of viewing the world.

Thank you for joining me on this journey through time and complex ideas about truth, language, technology, and persuasion. Rhetoric has been suppressed and pushed out of Western education because it's a powerful discipline that empowers citizens to be critical thinkers. People in power don't want you to have rhetoric. But now you do. Or, at least, you have a start. Help revive the art of rhetoric by talking about it; asking big questions; being unafraid to question the credibility of a speaker and their credentials; and getting to the bottom of the lies, deception, and disinformation that run rampant through the world in both our digital and physical spaces. If we want to live in a world where we value the truth, we'll have to start at home in our own lives. No one else is going to do it for us.

Well, I must leave you, now. Godspeed, budding rhetorician. I wish you the best of luck, and a good, long adventure in your pursuit of the truth, wherever it may be found.

THAT'S WHAT LIBERAL EDUCATION IS ALL ABOUT:
HOW DO YOU COME TO TERMS WITH THE QUEST FOR
TRUTH AND GOODNESS AND BEAUTY IN SUCH A WAY
THAT YOU CAN ENGAGE IN DISAGREEMENT AND
STILL MEDIATE IT WITH RESPECT, BUT RECOGNIZE
THAT MUCH IS AT STAKE? IT'S NOT A GAME, IT'S NOT
A PUZZLE, TALKING ABOUT THE FUTURE AND
DESTINY OF THE SPECIES...

—CORNEL WEST [105]

## CHAPTER X

# Staying Rhetorical: A Short Bibliographical Essay

I here take some loose inspiration from the stylings of Philip Taylor in his *Munitions of the Mind: A History of Propaganda from the Ancient World to the Modern Day*, where he features a bibliographical essay at the end of his book to document his sources. I like this method for several reasons. While I have endeavored to provide sources and relevant commentary as I saw fit in endnotes, there is no doubt that a person who reads hundreds and thousands of monographs, articles, primary sources, and has lived through interesting historical experiences does quite a bit of synthesizing in the generation of a new text. A bibliographic essay helps to show what sources I am thinking about and bringing together, even when it might not be readily apparent to the reader. While this is not a perfect solution, either, it does provide an opportunity to give a narrative account of the many sources that I have come across over the years of my reading and thinking on this subject, and thus provides some jumping off points to readers who wish to further explore this topic and related texts.

Perhaps more than that, I think a bibliographical essay helps to show the timespan of research and the years of thinking that go into a project like this and helps to build its credibility while demonstrating the vast network of interconnected, interdisciplinary knowledge that is referenced in its creation. I hope some readers will find this useful, not only to continue reading about this topic and these themes, but perhaps to find inspiration for how they might approach their own research. It's a lifelong endeavor. It all starts with a lot of reading, thinking, and questioning.

I am first indebted to the classical rhetoricians such as George Kennedy's work *A New History of Classical Rhetoric* as the backbone of my understanding of the beginnings of rhetoric in Ancient Greece and his *Comparative Rhetoric: An Historical and Cross-Cultural Comparison* for its global perspectives. In the introductory rhetoric class I teach at university, I have often used James Williams's *An Introduction to Classical Rhetoric: Essential Readings*, which features spectacular essays to provide rich social, cultural, and scholarly context around the prominent classical rhetoricians. There are probably more inclusive and accessible textbooks to reference on classical rhetoric, such as *The Rhetoric of Western Thought: From the Mediterranean World to the Global Setting*, which I have also referenced. I learned new perspectives from Gerard A. Hauser's *Introduction to Rhetorical Theory* as a sort of armchair-philosopher's take on the whole of rhetoric. I have also, at times, made reference to Kennedy's *Classical Rhetoric & Its Christian and Secular Tradition* as well as the mighty *The Rhetorical Tradition* by Patricia Bizzell and Bruce Herzberg, which is unrivaled in its scope and weight and sits on my home office shelf as a go-to reference. I often make quick reference to ancient texts thanks to Project Gutenberg and the MIT Classics

Archive, both of which are freely available online. There is absolutely nothing wrong with reading ancient Greek texts from freely available online translations, though I still love libraries and we
could use them more often. I began my lifelong research more
than twenty years ago at the Peter White Public Library in Marquette, MI where I found the philosophy section as a teenager and
began to read Plato, Aristotle, Nietzsche, Heidegger, Wittgenstein,
Camus, Stephen Hawking, and many others.

Kate Rich and Cheryl Glenn have done extraordinary work
in bringing attention to the role of women in classical rhetoric, in
their *Women in the History of Rhetoric* published by the American Society for the History of Rhetoric. I made contact with Dr.
Roberta Binkley at Arizona State University while working on
this book, and she provided me with a copy of her excellent
book: *Enheduanna, Before God*. I came across the research of
Dr. Binkley through her work on an important edited collection,
*Rhetoric Before and Beyond the Greeks*. Indeed, there is still
much research to be done on pre-Greek rhetoric, comparative
rhetoric, women in rhetoric, and the suppressed voices of classical rhetorical history. Perhaps some of my readers will go on to
become scholars and shed more light on these still-developing
areas of investigation. As I state throughout the book, while the
ancient Greeks certainly formalized and "invented" rhetoric, or
so our history suggests, it is doubtless that people before ancient
Greeks were using communication strategies in propaganda and
disinformation very readily; of course, I have documented that in
this book with my exploration of Enheduanna's religious propaganda and poetry. Kennedy suggests that rhetoric is as old as we
are, as our species. Donna J. Haraway writes of a kind of animal
rhetoric in *When Species Meet*, and of course, the Cornell Orni-
thology Lab has documented what is essentially American crow

language. And for the record, I still wonder why dogs aren't ticklish. Life is too short for a person with questions.

While I began studying philosophy independently as a young, long-haired lad in the Upper Peninsula of Michigan—I was irritated that there was no public school curriculum for philosophy or much room for the great questions of human experience in the high school classroom—I eventually made my way to Roosevelt University in Chicago, Illinois, where I played gigs as a singer-songwriter and rode around the "L," taking notes and reading with the cityscape to amaze and excite my young mind. I listened to Fleet Foxes and Bon Iver, The Mountain Goats, and Neutral Milk Hotel, among other of the neo-folk artists who have, by now, steadily made their way into the annals of "dad rock." (They were really cool at the time.) From Neutral Milk Hotel, I always loved the lyric, "How strange it is to be anything at all," which I have felt encapsulates human experience rather nicely. At Roosevelt University I was inspired by my composition professor, Eric Plattner, who showed me that a classroom can be a conversation, and philosophy was alive and well. He once set a red coffee thermos down on a table at the end of class and challenged any of us to write a paper in which we explain how the thermos was, in fact, not red at all. Of course, I eagerly took the offer and began a simplistic paper on how color was merely perception, that we can't verify the subjective experience of others, that language is a mostly arbitrary construct, and so on. These are important thinking exercises. And I always felt at home when I was in the room with people who would dare—or bother—to ask such questions.

I finished my undergraduate studies at Northern Michigan University, where I read Russian literature and fell in love with Tolstoy, Dostoevsky, and Turgenev. I have read *War & Peace* several times, and *Anna Karenina* too many. Perhaps my greatest pleasure at NMU was reading Shakespeare with Dr. David Wood, who showed me that a professor can be warm, fun, and kind, and fairly warned me that the life of an academic was not particularly glorious nor luxurious—in fact, it is hardly even possible. My readers may not know that now, most American university courses are taught by adjuncts (about 70 percent of all US courses) who are horribly underpaid and often may not even have university-provided health insurance. I'm reminded of Tolkien's *The Lord of the Rings,* when Faramir comments about what a noble and fine place the Shire must be if they honor gardeners so highly. I wonder what it says about the US that we do not take very good care of our educators. I suppose that is a self-serving argument. To continue, Dr. Wood helped make Shakespeare make sense to me. Now, I can hardly imagine what I missed. Look at *Hamlet,* for example: ghosts, murder, revenge, existential catastrophe. You can't go wrong there. Between Roosevelt and NMU, I obtained a fair knowledge of Western history, literary theory and methods, English, American, and Russian literature, and something of composition pedagogy and rhetoric.

I was then accepted into a PhD program at Michigan Technological University in Rhetoric & Technical Communication. I started teaching multimodal composition at Michigan Technological University when I was fairly young, just twenty-one. I rented an abysmal apartment in an absolutely unsanitary and dilapidated late 1800s home, crooked and falling, on Elm Street. I still remember the feeling of a large house spider running across my back in the middle of the night. I was making less than $10,000 a year, not enough to live on, but received a full tuition waiver in exchange for teaching three classes per year (what we would call a 2-1 load, or two classes in the fall and one in the spring). I suppose it worked out in the end. At MTU, I read everything from Heidegger to Latour to Baudrillard to Derrida. I was instructed more closely in research methodologies and began publishing my work. I am still appreciative that Moe Folk and Shawn Apostel took an interest in my first academic work, a chapter-length contribution to their book, *Digital Ethos: Evaluating Computer-Mediated Communication* (IGI Global, 2012). It was a somewhat-eccentric piece, where I connect the study of rhetoric to musicology through the sonic world-building of video-game music. Throughout my doctoral studies, I read everything I could, from Baudelaire to Bogost, and I was introduced to several different methods of inquiry and interdisciplinary research, blending approaches from digital media theory, the philosophy of technology, classical rhetoric, and contemporary visual, digital, and non-discursive rhetoric. Dr. Scott Marratto, the phenomenal phenomenologist, provided us a deep reading of Plato's *Phaedrus*, which still informs my understanding of the dialogue to this day. Dr. Stefka Hristova helped me to see the relationship between the material and the immaterial, the "reality of the virtual," if you will, and was always supportive of my early research work. Also very supportive were Dr. Robert Johnson who helped me immensely with Plato and Aristotle and Dr. Karla Kitalong who helped me expand my thinking across disciplines and to think not just outside of the box but to connect ideas with other boxes and intellectual traditions.

After obtaining a PhD, I involved myself in industry work, and I began to see how ethics had become entirely separated from messaging in the practices of digital marketing and the online world. I learned how to use social media platforms to target users with highly tailored advertisements based on their interests, geography, online behaviors, and demographic data, and developed persuasive content fitted to them. This was frightening to me—here, I found myself doing the very thing Plato warned against. I was persuading for a paycheck. I was using technology and tools to change reality in a way that made my conscience tell me to stop. I knew I had to get back to teaching, to help others understand the gravity and danger of digital tools and technologies.

Now, I'm Associate Professor of Writing at the University of Wisconsin – Superior, and I read Plato, among many other things, with my students. Most important to me now are my students. They ask me exciting questions about what we are reading and never fail to surprise me. I read Plato's *Phaedrus* every year when it comes around again for me to teach it, and every time I read it, I learn something new. Sometimes I get a little tired of Aristotle, but I still learn new things from him, as well. I suppose this has painted a small picture of some of the works I have read that have inspired this book. There are many others, such as Marshall McLuhan, who famously wrote, "The medium is the message," or Lev Manovich, whose work helped me to understand the relationship between our computer technologies and film and the interconnected nature of media history. But I think going on too long with this exercise would bore the reader, so I will stop now. If you are interested in reading more about rhetoric and disinformation, I might recommend you check out some of the books and texts I have mentioned here, or throughout this book. There is always more to read and think about. Just don't forget to take a walk and look at some water or some trees along the way.

Remember, rhetoric is just as much something that you *do* as something that you read about. Rhetoric is not just the art of speaking well. It's a way of looking at the world—to analyze persuasive messages, to think about our audience, and to strengthen our arguments. It's passed down to us as an art form because there is no definitive quantitative science of persuasion. It's a field of study that asks big questions about language, ethics, truth, writing, and education. Rhetoric is everywhere: from the strategies of contemporary political social media advertising campaigns to the text messages we send every day. And the specific techniques of rhetoric are central to writing and literature, from metaphor and simile to anaphora and antithesis. "It was the best of times, it was the worst of times…" That's antithesis. That's rhetoric.

Rhetoric can be brought back to life, but we must actively talk about it, think about it, and manifest it in the way we interact with the world. Question everything. That's one place to start. Read a little more, and question everything. Don't be afraid of Plato and Aristotle. Don't be afraid to have a serious conversation about credibility, language, and persuasion. Don't be afraid to challenge others and their perspectives on reality and truth. Ultimately, it's going to be up to me and you to seek out the truth. Time has shown us that we can't trust big business, governments, advertisers, or political organizations to figure it out for us. We're on our own, left to our own faculties. So, strengthen those faculties as best as you can.

# Rhetorical Toolkit:
# A Glossary of Terms

Audience – In rhetorical studies, the audience is the recipient of a message or the intended listener of a speech or act of communication. An audience might be a single person or a collection of large groups of people. Messages are shaped in particular ways for particular audiences. For example, a political advertisement directed toward working-class voters might feature a politician wearing a hard hat or working outdoors to attempt to portray the candidate as being part of their group (see also Kenneth Burke's concept of "identification"). It is important to understand why we have been targeted as an audience. Marketers and communication strategists think about age, income level, educational background, religious and political affiliations, and many other identifiers when thinking strategically about audience.

Aristotle – Aristotle was a student of Plato and studied under him at The Academy until Plato's death. I like to joke that

Aristotle was a bit like a rebellious teenager in relation to the older Plato. Aristotle built on, and rejected, many of Plato's ideas, and from this split with Plato, he formed the basis for many fields of study which we still have today (such as biology and zoology). But Aristotle was also the first to show how a systematic method of investigation could be applied to multiple different subjects, laying down a kind of early scientific methodology. Like with Plato, it is hard to overstate the significant influence Aristotle has had on Western thought. His writings laid down a groundwork for subjects as diverse as rhetoric, ethics, philosophy, physics, and biology, and provided the world with a model for an empirical, observational study of the universe.

Artistic Appeals – Aristotle defined the artistic appeals in Book I of his work on *Rhetoric*. Ethos, pathos, and logos are the three artistic appeals. They can—and often are—used simultaneously in the construction of messages to have a particular effect on an audience. While Aristotle was primarily thinking about the construction of speeches, we now apply the artistic appeals to all forms of communication to help us analyze how they influence and persuade us. Briefly, ethos refers to character and credibility; pathos refers to appeals to our emotions; and logos refers to appeals to logic. These artistic (or "artificial") proofs are sometimes referred to as "The Rhetorical Triangle" or "The Rhetorical Appeals" and are commonly taught in passing reference in college freshman writing courses. Aristotle sets these three artistic proofs in contrast to inartistic proofs, which are facts or statistics that can be plainly stated. The artistic proofs, on the other hand, can be used to construct arguments where the plain facts of a matter are not enough. These are useful tools for analyzing advertisements and messages in our world—most simple arguments like advertisements feature one or more of the artistic proofs defined by Aristotle.

Disinformation – Disinformation is a form of communication that intentionally presents lies or a false representation of reality to an audience for an intended purpose. Disinformation has been cleverly applied in warfare for hundreds, maybe thousands, of years, and these cases make for good examples. During WWII, British intelligence officers placed letters and fake papers on a dead body that was then positioned to wash up onshore in Nazi-occupied Italy. The deception tactic was successful in tricking Nazi forces into thinking the Allies would invade Greece rather than their planned target of Sicily. But disinformation is also used by large corporations to sway public opinion, and by foreign governments to incite civil unrest. Disinformation has many purposes and many audiences. The primary difference between propaganda and disinformation is that disinformation is always deceitful, fake, or untrue, whereas propaganda is not always untrue. Propaganda can be based on facts and reality, while disinformation is, by definition, deceitful or untrue.

Misinformation – Misinformation is inaccurate or untrue information that spreads unknowingly or accidentally throughout a population, whether the medium is verbal or technological (such as on social media). Misinformation is untrue or inaccurate, and in this way, it is similar to disinformation. But, unlike disinformation, which is *intended* to disinform and deceive, misinformation can be unintentionally spread. For example, a person who is not well trained in evaluating the credibility of information might share an article on social media that they *believe to be* true, even if the information is not true.

"Fake News" – Fake News is a term that refers to information that is fabricated or untrue but is disguised as a reputable news article. It has become a common phrase for people to use—sometimes jokingly, sometimes seriously—to criticize any information that they believe to be untrue. Fake news, in the purest sense of the definition, would refer to media such as a website that is designed to look like a reputable news organization where the articles are fabricated, made up, or not fact-checked—blatant untruths. Also falling under this umbrella would be opinion pieces that are made to sound or look like genuine news reports. Some fake news can also appear on major networks and large organizations when anchors, journalists, producers, or executives push stories that are not based in reality or are deliberately designed to mislead audiences away from the truth or to push a particular narrative surrounding a story. (We often see news organizations truncate the scale of bar graphs, for example, to push a particular perspective.) In a sense, all "news" is fabricated—we should remember that news organizations are trying to sell advertising space, subscriptions, or other services and goods, and that the very action of choosing which stories to present to the public can shape the way we perceive reality. The "news" is just a singular presentation of reality. Do not let others dictate what you care about or what grabs your attention—think for yourself.

Propaganda – Propaganda can refer both to the artifacts as well as the process of distributing messages that are intended to cause

large numbers of people to commit to an action, think a particular way, or change their beliefs about a topic. Propaganda generally has a wide, public, non-specific audience and thus attempts
to appeal to simple, universal feelings and emotions using slogans or visual imagery. Some propaganda is obvious, such as
World War II-era posters with slogans like "Loose lips sink
ships," urging US citizens not to discuss news of the war for fear
of domestic spies learning about troop movements or other national secrets. Propaganda can also be more complex or indirect,
such as the printing of slogans or imagery on currency like paper
money, or in the purposeful use of architecture or public dis-
plays to have particular effects (such as in Nazi-era rallies). Propaganda is always rhetorical, or persuasive, in nature; it is
created to have a particular effect on a particular (though usually large) audience. Propaganda takes many forms beyond Nazi
rallies and wartime posters—it can manifest as complex, digital
strategies as well.

Rhetoric – Rhetoric is the art of persuasion. While the ancient
Greeks were mostly concerned with persuasive speech, rhetoric now encompasses the study of persuasive messaging
through any medium or technology. Many sub-fields of rhetoric—such as digital rhetoric and visual rhetoric—have grown
to include frameworks and methods for analyzing non-lin-
guistic (non-discursive) rhetoric. Or, as the author of this book
has put it: "Rhetoric is philosophy with legs." Rhetoric is the
toolkit that allows us to analyze the communication strategies
that others are using against us and encompasses a set of ethical questions about persuasion. For Aristotle, rhetoric was
"The faculty observing in any given case the available means
of persuasion." For Plato, rhetoric was a way of "directing the

soul by means of speech." These ideas are still with us, today, and help to show the value of rhetoric as a tool in fighting disinformation.

Meta-rhetoric – Meta-rhetoric is a slightly outdated term that refers to the study of the theory of the art of persuasion. For example, several ancient texts "take a step back" and attempt to theorize about rhetoric itself, such as Plato's *Phaedrus* and Aristotle's *Rhetoric*. More recently, meta-rhetoric is just lumped into the study of rhetoric, so that we can more simply say that rhetoric is both *the art of* and *the study of the art of* persuasion. When you're "doing rhetoric," you should also be engaged in meta-rhetorical thinking. In other words, to be a good rhetorician means also to think about the theory of rhetoric itself, why we persuade, the ethics of persuasion, and so on, and not just the tools and techniques that are used for effective communication. Just like Plato warned us, you must first be a philosopher, and only then should you be a rhetorician.

Rhetorical Analysis – Rhetorical analysis is the analysis of a text, object, medium, network, or other phenomenon with the purpose of understanding how it functions persuasively. For example, we might conduct a rhetorical analysis on a thirty-second YouTube video advertisement to try to understand what the advertisement has been crafted to make us think, feel, or believe, and then decode the specific ways that it has been crafted to do so. When analyzing a video advertisement, we might look at the language that is used (word choice, syntax, or rhetorical devices), the use of imagery and symbolism, the use of color, the use of videographic techniques like cuts, camera angles, pans, zooms, or post-processing effects, the use of music, or the use of inartistic and artistic appeals (ethos, pathos, and logos). This is not an exhaustive list—really this is just scratching the surface of rhetorical analysis.

Inartistic Appeals – Per Aristotle, inartistic appeals are rhetorical appeals to facts. Aristotle sets up the inartistic appeals in contrast to the artistic appeals of ethos, pathos, and logos. We see inartistic appeals in contemporary political speeches and even advertisements. For example, we might see a commercial for a product that lists its technical specifications or price point. These simple facts about the product are inartistic appeals and carry rhetorical power. (Companies think about the rhetoric of the price point of their products in terms of its marketing and how it will relate to competition.) Often, inartistic appeals can share blurred lines with disinformation, such as with many food brands who use poorly regulated terms like "cage-free." (This phenomenon is called greenwashing.) Commonly, we see individuals and organizations telling plain lies and attempting to pass them off as verifiable, inartistic appeals. People who lie about dire human issues and the serious matters of life, especially when they do so for personal gain, are—in the author's opinion—among the evilest, most morally bankrupt of all humans.

Kairos – Kairos is the ancient Greek concept of non-linear time, as opposed to Kronos. In rhetoric, kairos is all about timing. For example, Dr. Martin Luther King Jr.'s famous "I Have a Dream" speech would not have had such a tremendous impact if he had delivered those lines on a street corner on a rainy day in Kansas City in 1931. But because the speech was delivered at the height of the American Civil Rights Movement, in Washington D.C., at an enormous peaceful protest, it was an opportune time in the broader sense of history. The social energy and cultural moment aided to make it so successful a speech. Advertisers always think about time. They try to figure out the best time of day to send an e-mail campaign to get you to buy a product and are always trying to hitch a ride along with viral trends, news of the day, and cultural moments. Keep an eye out.

Socrates – Socrates is the quintessential philosopher, who persistently asks us to question everything. Socrates did not write down anything himself, but his disciple Plato wrote many dialogues in which Socrates is a character. Socrates seems to have been a stonecutter by trade, and was often described as a "gadfly" for his sometimes irritating lines of questioning. Let's be honest; it's uncomfortable to have your values and worldview questioned by others! But Socrates persisted in asking questions of everyone he spoke with, to try to expose how little we know about ourselves and the world. He was put to death for this, eventually. Fortunately, a death sentence is no longer a realistic occupational hazard for most rhetoricians and philosophers. In my opinion, Socrates had the right "spirit" of philosophy. It's an endeavor of asking questions. Big questions. Why are we here? What does it mean to live a good life? What should we do with our time on this planet? Where are we, anyway? Socrates was unafraid to question authority and poke holes in others' ideas.

The Socratic Method – Socrates liked to ask questions to find out the true nature of the world and peoples' beliefs. In today's language, Socrates might ask a question like, "What do you think is the purpose of government?" To which you might reply, "To administer justice." Of course, Socrates would then ask you: "When you say justice, what do you mean by that word?" And you might respond, "To keep the laws and make sure everything is in order." Socrates would then follow up with something like, "But surely there are some laws which are not just, and some that are. How do we differentiate between them? And when you say order, what do you mean by order?" Many citizens of Athens found this rather irritating, and there were even satirical portrayals of Socrates in stage comedies like Aristophanes's *The Clouds* which caricatured Socrates. Still, today, we recognize Socrates as being representative of the very heart of philosophy. As contemporary philosopher Slavoj Zizek puts it, the role of philosophy is "to ask questions."

The Socratic Problem – The "Socratic Problem" exists because Socrates did not write anything down (or if he did, it does not survive). Instead, we only see Socrates as a character in Plato's dialogues. Thus, it is basically impossible to separate the fictional, characterized version of Socrates that Plato wrote down from the real, living Socrates who walked the streets of Athens. It's very likely that Plato injected many of his own ideas and perspectives into the character of Socrates throughout his many dialogues. However, some argue that Plato's dialogues are more like written records of actual conversations rather than fictional dialogues. The truth of the matter probably lies somewhere in between these two extremes. (You can attempt such an exercise yourself: go have a dinner or a stroll with a couple of friends and have a long chat about life, love, and the meaning of the universe. Later, sit down and see if you can write out the conversation as it unfolded. You might get some of the details and salient arguments fleshed out, but it won't be an exact representation of what was said.)

Gorgias – I call Gorgias the "Rockstar Rhetorician," as he was one of the most celebrated orators of his time, and regularly traveled about the ancient Mediterranean to deliver speeches to dazzled audiences. One of his showstopping, go-to speeches was "The Encomium of Helen," in which he lays out an argument for why we should not blame Helen for the Trojan War. Some view this as one of the earliest examples of a feminist text. Though Gorgias gives us plenty to think about, he represents the kind of Sophist that Plato spent much of his life working against. We see at the end of "The Encomium of Helen" how Gorgias explains that, if he had cared to do so, he could have just as easily entertained himself by making the exact opposite argument: that instead of arguing in favor of Helen, he could have just as easily blamed her. Plato hated this kind of Sophist, who went about teaching people how to make "lesser causes seem the greater" and use language to weave webs of deceit.

Narrative Rhetoric – Narrative rhetoric is the use of stories, myths, fictions, and other forms of narrative to make an argument or attempt to persuade. For example, a parent might use the story of Santa Claus to modify the behavior of their children: "If you don't behave yourself properly, then Santa won't bring you any presents." More broadly, narratives are used to influence and persuade in films, video games, and even economically and socially at large scales. Consider how a news organization can shape the narrative around an issue by presenting a particular perspective, and in turn, shape peoples' perception of that issue. American news organizations have, for many years, put forth a narrative about the millennial generation: that they are lazy, work less, and are somehow inferior to previous generations. However, there are no studies that support this—in fact, Millennials generally work longer hours for less pay (and have less buying power when it comes to most goods, services, and even home-buying) when compared to both their parents and grandparents. Myths, stories, and narratives can alter our perception of reality. Humans have been telling stories for tens of thousands of years, and maybe longer, and stories are a defining element of human experience—but stories can also be used for malevolent purposes, such as how Hitler crafted a false narrative about Jewish people being responsible for the economic issues in Germany following World War I.

Procedural Rhetoric – Procedural rhetoric is Ian Bogost's theory that processes and procedures can be persuasive. While Bogost mainly uses video games to explain this theory, analog and physical procedures and processes can also be persuasive. Rules can be used to make arguments and can be automated algorithmically. For example, imagine an algorithm that was designed to sort through a list of organ recipients and put them in order of who should receive their organ donations. How would it be written: to favor those with the lowest income, or the youngest patients, or those with the best chance of survival? Whichever method we choose, we are making some argument about how we value life, and we are creating a procedure that will have a very real impact on the world. Now, imagine the many algorithms that determine which content ends up in your social media feed or which YouTube videos are recommended to you. These algorithms often spread misinformation and disinformation rampantly.

Enheduanna – Enheduanna, an ancient priestess-poet, is the world's first named author whose works have survived to present day. Her poems help us to understand early rhetoric before the ancient Greeks. In Enheduanna's works, we see many rhetorical techniques which still survive today, including anaphora or antithesis. Much new scholarship is available on Enheduanna, though in my estimation, it is dangerously incomplete. Enheduanna seems to have been primarily a religious propagandist in service of the empire of King Sargon I, her father. Reading Enheduanna's poetry in celebration of her accomplishments without the broader context would be like celebrating the rhetoric of Hitler's speeches without acknowledging his extraordinary crimes against humanity.

Plato – Plato was a student of Socrates and would go on to include Socrates in his dialogues. The dialogues are best understood, not as actual records of conversations, but as fictional works—though there is some gray area, and we can't be certain to what extent some of these dialogues may have resembled real conversations that took place in ancient Athens. They are likely idealized versions that both express Socrates's teachings and channel Plato's own thinking. Plato is one of the most important thinkers of human history. He was our first psychologist, the man who set the wisdom of Socrates down in written record for future generations, and a great teacher who founded The Academy and shaped human education for thousands of years to come. Plato's significance on Western thinking cannot be overstated. In this book, we primarily focused on Plato's dialogue *Phaedrus*, which explores themes of divine madness, love, the relationship between rhetoric and philosophy, the relationship between rhetoric and truth, Sophistry, the technology of writing, the nature of the soul, and other important ideas.

# Acknowledgments

Many thanks to Lydia Stevens at Urano Publishing who understood clearly the vision of this book, and supported me throughout the journey.

I am very indebted to my most lovely wife, Kendra, who continues to make time and space for me to write, even when it's difficult. Every day I feel lucky that we found each other.

My beautiful children, Nova, Fox, and Juniper, keep me happy, smiling, and busy in the good way. My house is my home, and full of good things. The dogs, Willie and Sadie, are good dogs, and the cats, Lola and Leo, are good cats.

My parents, Vicki and Bill Lawrence, have supported me in my life's pursuit of unexpected adventures.

My colleagues in the Department of Writing, Language, and Literature at the University of Wisconsin – Superior are very good and smart people, and I have benefited incalculably just from being around them as often as I am.

# About the Author

Daniel William Lawrence, PhD is Associate Professor of Writing at the University of Wisconsin – Superior. He received his PhD in Rhetoric & Technical Communication with a specialization in Digital Media Theory from Michigan Technological University and a BA in English from Northern Michigan University.

He grew up in Michigan's Upper Peninsula and now lives in northern Wisconsin with his wife and three children. He is a faculty member of the Department of Writing, Language, and Literature at UW –Superior and teaches courses such as Introduction to Rhetoric, Advanced Rhetoric: Theory and Practice, Technical Writing, and Digital Writing on the UW – Superior campus and in the fully online BA in Writing program.

Visit danlawrenceauthor.com to learn more.

# About the Author

# Image Attribution

Figure 1: "Map of Ancient Athens": "The ancient world, from the earliest times to 800 A.D." 1913. Page 226. From *Internet Archive Book Image*. Public domain image. Retrieved November 2022 from: https://flickr.com/photos/internetarchivebookimages/14758260096/in/photolist-ou8Wyh-ovJrP2-oeQoj7-oeFhz9-ov1JVH-otx33y-ovVebV-ouq3np-oxh1Ai-ow8Bch-otHdUU-owiS3N-ouw3NH-oeZjar-owiKX4-ot6jXY-owgaWw-ovZF4w-oy6k72-oviU4Q-oupPDP-ovY6zE-ovNN93-oeJjhG-oeL6TE-ovWFWg-ovYRDu-ouPx9B-oeJ8uF-ovPDSo-oujPbY-owF4pz-oem3ms-owksPE-2kVyP6z-2jLM9Kv-cBN9ru-ovRdma-owrEmD-ow1HGL-oeJ8Nr-oxYBFP-oxcVtn-ouTARj-Ki843e-oxYEFg-ouQGKP-oxXjJe-oeJhBN-owiYz5/

Figure 2: "Drawing of Ancient Athens": "The eastern nations and Greece." 1917. Page 236. From *Internet Archive Book Image*. Public domain image. Retrieved November 2022 from: https://flickr.com/photos/internetarchivebookimages/14786964603/in/photolist-owF4pz-oem3ms-owksPE-2kVyP6z-2jLM9Kv-cBN9ru-ovRdma-owrEmD-ow1HGL-oeJ8Nr-oxYBFP-oxcVtn-ouTARj-Ki843e-oxYEFg-ouQGKP-oxXjJe-oeJhBN-owiYz5-oxArxg-oyc4hz-ouQDWx-oeukMA-ovXKuN-oevh2K-oubZF3-ouD12X-oudTzw-otHek3-ouMX7F-oeCXpv-oxPsKk-ovHfon-2iWRVFM-6bJAEd-KhKSEN-

oxCkZi-oeYQMc-ovizy3-KeB1uM-oeQynA-a81Ne8-oeHVA1-oeF4mB-
ow4769-vNEyC1-ov3HDb-owhbUT-oxLZ1X-owGasp/

Figure 3: Bacon, Henry. "General View of the Acropolis at Sunset."
Smithsonian Digital Collections, Smithsonian American Art Museum.
1927.5.5. Public Domain. Retrieved November 2022 from: https://
americanart.si.edu/artwork/general-view-acropolis-sunset-801

Figure 4: Salvator, Rosa. "Plato teaching at his Academy: a gathering of
students, among them possibly Aristotle." Wikimedia Commons. Public
Domain. Retrieved November 2022 from: https://commons.wikimedia.
org/wiki/File:Plato_teaching_at_his_Academy;_a_gathering_of_
students,_amon_Wellcome_V0006666.jpg

Figure 5: Powers, Hiram. "19th Century Statue of a Greek Slave."
Smithsonian American Art Museum, 1968.155.109 - Modeled 1841-
1843. Public Domain. Retrieved November 2022 from: https://library.
si.edu/

Figure 6: Bust of Socrates. Anderson, Domenico. "Artistical rendition of
Socrates, called 'A man named Socrates.'" Public Domain. Retrieved
November 2022 from: https://commons.wikimedia.org/wiki/
File:Anderson,_Domenico_(1854-1938)_-_n._23185_-_Socrate_
(Collezione_Farnese)_-_Museo_Nazionale_di_Napoli.jpg

Figure 7: Raphael, (Raffaello Sanzio da Urbino) "The School of Athens."
Fresco at the Raphael Rooms, Apostolic Palace, Vatican City. 1509-
1511. Public Domain. Retrieved November 2022 from: https://
commons.wikimedia.org/wiki/File:%22The_School_of_Athens%22_by_
Raffaello_Sanzio_da_Urbino.jpg

Figure 8: Weissinger, Matt. "A Ford F-150 Raptor on the Road." CC0.
Retrieved April, 2023 from: https://www.pexels.com/photo/a-ford-f-
150-raptor-on-the-road-10306505/.

# Notes

## Notes to Introduction

1. Tolkien, J.R.R. The Two Towers: Being the Second Part of the Lord of the Rings. Del Rey, Mass Market Paperback Edition. 2018. (Orig. 1954).

2. Gramlich, John. "10 facts about Americans and Facebook." Pew Research Center. June 1, 2021. https://www.pewresearch.org/facttank/2021/06/01/facts-about-americans-and-facebook/

3. Tolkein, J.R.R. Ibid.

4. Jefferson, Thomas. *Monticello and Thomas Jefferson Foundation.* Retrieved 2022 from https://tjrs.monticello.org/archive/search/quotes?keys=&sort_bef_combine=field_tjrs_date_value+ASC&field_tjrs_categorization_tid%5B%5D=2174&field_tjrs_date_value_1%5Bvalue%5D%5Bdate%5D=&field_tjrs_date_value2_1%5Bvalue%5D%5Bdate%5D=&_ga=2.268244750.1452851866.1658162150-947895285.1658162150

5. Breakstone, J., et al. *Students' civic online reasoning: A national portrait.* Stanford History Education Group. 2019. Retrieved from

https://sheg.stanford.edu/students-civic-online-reasoning. See also Breakstone, J., et al. (2017). *The challenge that's bigger than fake news: Civic reasoning in a social media environment.* American Educator, 14(3). Retrieved from https:// www.aft.org/ae/fall2017/ mcgrew_ortega_breakstone_wineburg.

6. Devitt, James and Kelly, B. Rose. "Fake News Shared by Very Few, But Those Over 65 More Likely to Pass on Such Stories, New Study Finds" https://spia.princeton.edu/news/fake-news-shared-very-few-those-over-65-more-likely-pass-such-stories-new-study-finds

7. West, Cornel. "Speaking Truth to Power." Lecture delivered at MIT. February 8, 2018. https://www.youtube.com/watch?v=-Bc6TRjptKI

## Notes to Chapter One

8. Gorgias. *Encomium of Helen.* Translated by George Kennedy. I've come across plenty of different copies of the ancient texts in my life, but I can recommend the solid anthology by Williams, James D. *An Introduction to Classical Rhetoric: Essential Readings.* I have taught from this textbook for several years and find it a good starting point. Wiley-Blackwell, 2009.

9. Gorgias. Ibid.

10. Chomsky, Noam and Herman, Edward. *Manufacturing Consent: The Political Economy of the Mass Media.* 1988.

11. "McDougal v. Fox News Network, LLC." United States District Court, Southern District of New York. 2020. https://law.justia.com/ cases/federal/district-courts/new-york/ nysdce/1:2019cv11161/527808/39/

12. Heidegger, Martin. "The Question Concerning Technology." Martin Heidegger: Basic Writings. Edited by David Krell. Harper & Row. 1977. Original 1954.

## Notes to Chapter Two

13. Bitzer, Lloyd. "The Rhetorical Situation." *Philosophy & Rhetoric.* 1.1. 1968.

14. Bitzer. Ibid.

15. Dittmann, M. "Standing tall pays off, study finds." https://www.apa. org/monitor/julaug04/standing

16. Mehic, Adrian. "Student beauty and grades under in-person and remote teaching." https://www.sciencedirect.com/science/article/pii/ S016517652200283X

17. Kennedy, George. *Comparative Rhetoric: An Historical and Cross-Cultural Introduction.* Oxford University Press. 1997. (17)

18. Kennedy, George. *Comparative Rhetoric: An Historical and Cross-Cultural Introduction.* Oxford University Press. 1997. (3-4)

19. Chomsky, Noam. *Media Control: The Spectacular Achievements of Propaganda.* Seven Stories Press, 2nd Edition. 2002. 24.

20. Allyn, Bobby. "Researchers: Nearly Half of Accounts Tweeting About Coronavirus are Likely Bots." May 20, 2020. https://www.npr.org/ sections/coronavirus-live-updates/2020/05/20/859814085/researchers-nearly-half-of-accounts-tweeting-about-coronavirus-are-likely-bots

21. Dunlop, John. "Aleksandr Dugin's Foundations of Geopolitics" (PDF). Demokratizatsiya: The Journal of Post-Soviet Democratization. Institute for European, Russian and Eurasian Studies, George Washington University. January 31, 2004.

22. Kennedy, George. Ibid.

23. Lincoln, Abraham & Roe, Merwin (Editor). Speeches and Letters of Abraham Lincoln, 1832-1865. "From an Address before the Young Men's Lyceum of Springfield, Illinois. January 27, 1837." Project Gutenberg. https://www.gutenberg.org/files/14721/14721-h/14721-h.htm#04

## Notes to Chapter Three

24. Plato. *Phaedrus*. Alexander Nehamas and Paul Woodruff, Translators. Hackett Publishing Company. 1995. 260e. Originally written circa 370 BCE. I find the Nehamas and Woodruff translation to be very readable, beautiful, and salient compared to the publicly available Benjamin Jowett translation, which is stiff and archaic. Jowett translated in the last few years of the 1800s, and seems to have tried to give Plato a kind of noble, antiquated feeling with archaic style. Jowett is still readable, but if you can get a copy of the Nehamas and Woodruff, then I recommend it more highly for reading Plato. And who knows, perhaps another translator will come along and do an even better job. I would love to see Plato masterfully translated for a new generation. Or maybe to see Platonic dialogues acted out like short, serialized streaming films? That would be cool. Very cool.

25. Plato. *Phaedrus*. 260c-260d. Ibid.

26. Hesiod's *Theogony*, dated to around 700 BCE

27. And for that matter, classicist and rhetorician George Kennedy suggests that many technical elements of formal rhetoric were present in ancient literature far before they were even put into description in his worthwhile *A New History of Classical Rhetoric*.

28. Berquist et al, *The Rhetoric of Western Thought: From the Mediterranean World to the Global Setting*. Kendall Hunt Publishing. 2020.

29. Plato's *Republic*, Book 7

30. Like any scholarly detail, there is worthwhile debate surrounding the numbers. I'm not an expert in ancient populations, so I'm intentionally a bit vague, here, as to not be inaccurate. There were some thirty thousand land-owning, wealthy males who would have participated in the democratic process. Estimates vary for fourth

century population of ancient Athens, but it was likely somewhere around 250,000-300,000 citizens based on our best current interpretations.

31. I openly paraphrase many observations, here, from the excellent "Introduction" to *Five Great Dialogues* by Louise Ropes Loomis in the very well known Benjamin Jowett translations published 1942, Walter J. Black, Inc. The Jowett translations are solid standards and are widely available, even on the Internet Classics Archive or Project Gutenberg, for readers who would like more of a taste of the primary sources.

32. This core human conflict between order and chaos (manifested as liberalism and conservatism) is problematically, though sometimes artfully, communicated in controversial clinical psychologist Dr. Jordan Peterson's recent book, *Beyond Order*.

33. Peterson, Jordon. Ibid.

34. Though more astute and careful readers will recognize in *Protagoras* as well as in *Phaedrus* that there are elements of romantic, pederastic conversation between speakers in the dialogue, scholars debate endlessly the extent to which it is unethical and creepy. It is probably both, at times, and maybe worse, at other times.

35. Kenneth Burke, *The Philosophy of Literary Form: Studies in Symbolic Action* 3rd ed. 1941. University of California Press, 1973

36. Burke, Kenneth. Ibid.

37. Plato. *Phaedrus*. Benjamin Jowett, Translator. MIT Classics Archive. Retrieved 2022. http://classics.mit.edu/Plato/phaedrus.html

38. For an especially helpful breakdown of the structure of the dialogue *Phaedrus*, I recommend the publicly available notes of Robert Cavalier from Carnegie Mellon University at: http://caae.phil.cmu.edu/ Cavalier/80250/Plato/Phaedrus/Phaedrus.html. In matter of content, though, we can see how Cavalier does not focus on the same themes

that we are most interested in, here, namely speech and truth, or the theme of rhetoric and its relationship to philosophy. Cavalier in his notes is more interested in *Eros*, which is not what we have time to discuss, here, but is fascinating in its own right. What is more universal than love?

## Notes to Chapter Four

39. Plato. *Phaedrus*. Nehamas and Woodruff, Translators. Hackett Publishing Company. 1995. 259e.

40. Plato. *Phaedrus*. Ibid. 260d.

41. The term "flow" comes from Csikszentmihalyi, Mihaly (1975). *Beyond Boredom and Anxiety: Experiencing Flow in Work and Play*

42. Cavalier, Robert. Ibid.

43. Plato. *Phaedrus*. Benjamin Jowett, Translator. Ibid.

44. See the excellent *Touched with Fire: Manic-Depressive Illness and the Artistic Temperament* by Kay Redfield Jamison for an engaging and thorough treatment of this ancient theme of madness and creativity. Also interesting, on the related topic of creativity in writing and substance abuse, is Olivia Laing's *The Trip to Echo Spring: On Writers and Drinking*.

45. Mary B. Schoen-Nazarro has written on Plato's and Aristotle's differing approaches to music in "Plato and Aristotle on the Ends of Music," Lavalthéologique et philosophique, 34(3), 261–273. 1978.

46. Plato. *Phaedrus*. Jowett, Translator. Ibid.

47. Plato. *Phaedrus*. Jowett, Translator. Ibid.

48. Plato. *Phaedrus*. Jowett, Translator. Ibid.

# Notes to Chapter Five

49.  Enheduanna. "The Hymn to Inanna." Translated by Jane Hirshfield. https://www.poetryfoundation.org/poems/157578/from-the-hymn-to-inanna

50.  Enheduanna. Ibid.

51.  Science Movie Club: "Arrival." https://www.npr.org/transcripts/901705799

52.  Echlin, Kim. *Inanna: A New English Version. (p. 5)*

53. Echlin, Kim. Ibid.

54.  Taylor, Philip M. *Munitions of the Mind: A History of Propaganda from the Ancient World to the Modern Era.* (21)

55.  Taylor. Ibid.19

56.  Taylor. Ibid 19-20

57.  Enheduanna. "The Hymn to Inanna." Ibid.

58. Taylor, Philip. Ibid.

59.  Fallis, Don. "What Is Disinformation?" Library Trends, vol. 63, no. 3, Johns Hopkins University Press, 2015, pp. 401–26, https://doi.org/10.1353/lib.2015.0014.

60.  Kennedy, George. *Comparative Rhetoric.* 132

61.  Kennedy, George. Ibid. 132-133.

62.  Kennedy, George. Ibid. 133

63.  Kennedy, George. Ibid. 138

64.  Chomsky, Noam. *Media Control: The Spectacular Achievements of Propaganda.* Ibid. 38-39

65.  Chomsky, Noam. Ibid. 40

66. Enheduanna. Ibid.

67. https://www.whitehouse.gov/state-of-the-union-2022/

68. *Beowulf*. Poetry Foundation. Retrieved 2022. https://www.
poetryfoundation.org/poems/43521/beowulf-old-english-version

## Notes to Chapter Six

69. Aristotle. *Rhetoric*. Translated by W. Rhys Roberts. MIT Internet
Classics Archive. Orig. 350 BCE. http://classics.mit.edu/Aristotle/
rhetoric.1.i.html

70. Aristotle. Ibid.

71. https://poetrysociety.org.uk/poems/the-st-crispins-day-speech-from-
henry-v/

72. https://www.poetryfoundation.org/poems/56972/speech-once-more-
unto-the-breach-dear-friends-once-more

73. "Noah S. Sweat." Wikipedia.org. Retrieved 2022. https://
en.wikipedia.org/wiki/Noah_S._Sweat#cite_ref-clar_2-0

74. Smith, Thomas. (Smith Advertising Agency.) *Successful Advertising:
Its Secrets Explained by Smith's Advertising Agency*. 21st Edition.
Original 1885. Retrieved in 2022: https://ia801905.us.archive.org/27/
items/successfuladvert00smit/successfuladvert00smit.pdf

75. I have taken here for my subject of analysis the following
advertisement: "The 2022 Ford F-150®: Tougher and Smarter | F-150 |
Ford :30." The Ford Motor Company. YouTube. Retrieved in 2022:
https://youtu.be/tfxPbpCymNg

76. Quintilian. *Institutes of Oratory*. https://kairos.technorhetoric.net/
stasis/2017/honeycutt/quintilian/2/chapter15.html

## Notes to Chapter Seven

77. Quintilian. Ibid.

78. "Ezekial 18." New International Version (NIV) Bible. Hosted by MIT Classics Archive. Retrieved from: http://web.mit.edu/jywang/www/cef/Bible/NIV/NIV_Bible/EZEK+18.html

79. Wilson & Arnold have a wonderful 16-point *topoi* system which seems quite universal and widely applicable to me. I think it is the best that I have seen. I received it through Gerard Hauser's work on rhetoric.

80. Transcripts retrieved from *The Commission on Presidential Debates (CPD)* in 2022: https://www.debates.org/voter-education/debate-transcripts/october-22-2020-debate-transcript/

81. Transcripts retrieved from *The Commission on Presidential Debates (CPD)* in 2022: https://www.debates.org/voter-education/debate-transcripts/october-22-2020-debate-transcript/

82. Transcripts retrieved from *The Commission on Presidential Debates (CPD)* in 2022: https://www.debates.org/voter-education/debate-transcripts/october-22-2020-debate-transcript/

83. McLuhan, Marshall. *The Medium is the Massage. An Inventory of Effects*. Bantam Books. 1967. Also see McLuhan's *Understanding Media: The Extensions of Man*. 1964. McLuhan is tricky, but the basic idea of "the medium is the message" is that the content of a medium is incidental. It doesn't matter so much *what* we are doing on our smartphones—what is more significant in McLuhan's theory is that we have smartphones at all, that we use them three or more hours a day, the effects that the medium has on us and the way we perceive and interact with the world and each other. Granted, most modern media theorists find some in-between area—both the content and the medium are significant and persuasive.

## Notes to Chapter Eight

84. Plato. *Phaedrus*. Ibid.

85. Heidegger, Martin."The Question Concerning Technology." Ibid.

86. Gibbon, Edward. *The Decline and Fall of the Roman Empire*. This massive work is available freely on Project Gutenberg, and I can attest it makes for good reading before bed. Of course there have been many advances in archaeology, anthropology, history, and a variety of other fields since the time of Gibbon's writing, but it remains singular in its sweeping coverage of ancient Rome from the Age of the Antonines to the fall of Constantinople. There's really nothing quite like it.

87. Haraway, Donna. "A Cyborg Manifesto." 1985.

88. Heidegger, Martin. "The Question Concerning Technology." *Martin Heidegger: Basic Writings*. Edited by David Krell. Harper & Row. 1977. Original 1954.

89. See the UGA Library's "Early History of the Microphone" for a quick history of the device: https://digilab.libs.uga.edu/scl/exhibits/show/steel_vintage_mics/mic_early_history#:~:text=Alexander%20Graham%20Bell%20patented%20the%20first%20microphone%20in%201876. A set of photographs shows early broadcasters using lamp shades to cover the microphone to help those who were afraid of the new technology.

90. Adgate, Brad. "Agencies Agree; 2021 Was a Record Year for Ad Spending, With More Growth Expected in 2022." Forbes.com. Retrieved March 10, 2023. https://www.forbes.com/sites/bradadgate/2021/12/08/agencies-agree-2021-was-a-record-year-for-ad-spending-with-more-growth-expected-in-2022/?sh=4a44db5b7bc6

91. https://certifiedhumane.org/9-disappointing-facts-chipotle/

92. Bogost, Ian. *Persuasive Games: The Expressive Power of Video Games*. MIT Press. 2007.

## Notes to Chapter Nine

93. Plato. *Phaedrus*. Ibid.

94. Burke. Kenneth. Ibid.

95. Chomsky, Noam. *Media Control: The Spectacular Achievements of Propaganda*. Ibid. Page 9.

96. Chomsky, Noam. Ibid. Page 10.

97. Taylor, Philip. Ibid. 4.

98. Taylor, Philip, Ibid. 5.

99. Garsten, Bryan. *Saving Persuasion: A Defense of Rhetoric and Judgment*. Harvard University Press. 2009. Page 2.

100. Garsten. Ibid. 3.

101. Plato. *Phaedrus*. Jowett, Translator. Ibid. This is near the end of the dialogue in the famous "Myth of Theuth" section which deals with writing as a technology and a critique of writing vs. the dialogic process.

102. Feynman, Richard. *Sure You're Joking, Mr. Feynman!* W. W. Norton & Company. 1997. 123-126

103. Feynman. Ibid.126-127

104. Plato. *Apology*. Benjamin Jowett, translator. See below for more detail on other Plato references throughout the text. http://classics.mit.edu/Plato/apology.html

## Notes to Chapter Ten

105. "Speaking Truth to Power." Lecture delivered at MIT. https://www.youtube.com/watch?v=-Bc6TRjptKI. For the other epigraphs and throughout the book, I quote directly from the source from various translations: Gorgias. *Encomium of Helen*. Plato. *Phaedrus, Republic,*

*and Apology.* The Benjamin Jowett translation is widely available online, though for *Phaedrus* I have referenced in places the Nehemas and Woodruff translation, Hackett Publishing Company, 1995. Aristotle. *On Rhetoric.* Cicero. *De Inventione.* Quintilian. *Institutio Oratorio.* Enheduanna. "The Hymn to Inanna," and others.